WITHDRAWN

This book is part of a series. The publisher will accept continuation orders which may be cancelled at any time and which provide for automatic billing and shipping of each title in the series upon publication. Please write for details.

Romania

THE UNFINISHED REVOLUTION

Steven D. Roper

harwood academic publishers
Australia • Canada • France • Germany • India
Japan • Luxembourg • Malaysia • The Netherlands
Russia • Singapore • Switzerland

Amsteldijk 166
1st Floor
1079 LH Amsterdam
The Netherlands

British Library Cataloguing in Publication Data

A catalogue record for this book is available from the British Library.

ISBN: 90-5823-028-7 (softcover)
ISSN: 1028-043X

TO MY PARENTS JAMES AND SHARON AND IN MEMORY
OF MY BROTHER KEVIN.

TABLE OF CONTENTS

CHRONOLOGY

1859	The principalities of Moldavia and Wallachia form a union.
1866	The United Principalities adopt a constitutional monarchy.
1878	The Treaty of Berlin recognizes the independence of the United Principalities.
1881	The United Principalities become a kingdom.
1918	The Old Kingdom unifies with Transylvania, Bukovina and Bessarabia to form Greater Romania.
1921	The Romanian Communist Party is founded.
1933	Gheorghe Gheorghiu-Dej organizes the Grivita strike and is imprisoned.
1940	The Soviet Union annexes Bessarabia and Northern Bukovina as part of the Molotov–Ribbentrop Pact. King Carol abdicates, and Marshal Ion Antonescu is appointed president of the Council of Ministers.
1944	The Soviet army enters Romania, and Marshal Antonescu is overthrown by a coup.
1945	Gheorghiu-Dej is named party first secretary.
1947	The monarchy is abolished and the Romanian People's Democracy is established.
1952	Ana Pauker and Vasile Luca are purged from the Romanian Workers' Party.
1953	Gheorghiu-Dej is named president of the Council of Ministers.
1958	Soviet troops are removed from Romania.
1965	Gheorghiu-Dej dies. Nicolae Ceausescu is named party general secretary.
1968	Ceausescu denounces the Soviet invasion of Czechoslovakia.
1981	Ceausescu implements an economic austerity plan.
1989	Ceausescu and his wife Elena are executed. The National Salvation Front is formed.
1990	In national elections, Ion Iliescu is elected president, and Petre Roman is named prime minister.
1991	The Romanian constitution is ratified. Theodor Stolojan replaces Roman as prime minister. The Democratic Convention of Romania is formed.
1992	In national elections, Iliescu is re-elected president and Nicolae Vacariou is named prime minister.
1993	Romania signs an association agreement with the European Union.
1996	Romania signs a friendship treaty with Hungary. In national elections, Emil Constantinescu is elected president, and Victor Ciorbea is named prime minister.
1998	Radu Vasile replaces Ciorbea as prime minister.

PREFACE

In the early 1990s, a number of books were published that examined the transition from the Ceausescu regime to the National Salvation Front. At that time, there was a great deal of speculation concerning the origins of the Romanian revolution. Many questioned whether Romania had experienced a revolution or simply a coup. For example, the title of Nestor Ratesh's *Romania: The Entangled Revolution*[1] pointed to both the importance and to the mystery surrounding the revolution. A decade later, many of these same questions concerning the revolution still persist. Rather than focus on the origins of the revolution, I believe that it is important to remember the goals that inspired many Romanians to give their lives. I subtitled this book *The Unfinished Revolution* because of the political, economic and foreign policy goals of the revolution that have yet to be fulfilled. This book attempts to provide an overview of the development of Romanian policies since 1989 and to place these policies within the context of Romanian political culture and the politics and economics of the new East Europe. The ideology and the geography of Europe have fundamentally changed since 1989. Eastern Europe was an ideological concept as well as a geographical location, both of which no longer exist, and Romania is searching for its place in this new East Europe. Throughout the book, I refer to 'Eastern Europe' when describing events prior to 1989. I have provided the Romanian names of organizations mentioned in the text and also their Romanian acronyms of organizations. These acronyms are those to be found commonly in the Romanian press.

This book is indebted to a number of people. Although I did not know it at the time, the book began while I was an undergraduate in an Eastern European politics course at the University of North Carolina at Greensboro in the spring of 1989. The professor, William Crowther, stirred my interest in a region that I had never really thought about. His research focused on Romanian political development and influenced me to study the emerging Romanian post-communist institutions. More than any other professor or colleague, Bill has shaped the direction of my professional life. I also want to thank Jeff Chinn, Charles King, Robin Remington and Lavinia Stan.

---

1   Nestor Ratesh, *Romania: The Entangled Revolution.* (Westport, CT: Prager, 1991).

In Romania, I want to thank my colleagues and friends at Lucian Blaga University including, Rector Dumitru Ciocoi-Pop, Professor Eugen Gergely and Dr. Alexandru Huditeanu. They always provided me an intellectual home and the city of Sibiu was a wonderful base for my research. Although I had to make weekly train trips to Bucharest, it was a great pleasure to return to the beauty of Transylvania. Gabriel Badescu of Babes Bolyai University in Cluj was a very helpful in the final stages of this project with tracking down material. I also want to thank Ana Stroia for showing me what Romanian hospitality and friendship really means.

Several organizations have provided me the funds necessary to conduct research in Romania. I want to acknowledge the financial assistance of the American Council of Learned Societies, the Social Science Research Council, the United States Information Agency, the Romanian Fulbright Commission and the Institute for International Education. Also, I want to thank Mariana Stoian at the Romanian Cultural Center in New York for her invaluable assistance. The book has benefited from the suggestions of a reader for Harwood Academic Publishers.

Finally, I want to thank my wife Lilian Barria for all her patience and understanding.

GLOSSARY OF ABBREVIATIONS

CDR   Democratic Convention of Romania (*Conventia Democratica din Romania*)

FDSN   Democratic National Salvation Front (*Frontul Democrat al Salvarii Nationale*)

FSN   National Salvation Front (*Frontul Salvarii Nationale*)

GUF   Group for the Front's Unity (*Grupul pentru Unitatea Frontului*)

LAM   Legion of Archangel Michael (*Legiunea Arhanghelului Mihail*)

PAC   Civic Alliance Party (*Partidul Aliantei Civice*)

PCR   Romanian Communist Party (*Partidul Comunist Roman*)

PD   Democratic Party (*Partidul Democrat*)

PD FSN   Democratic Party National Salvation Front (*Partidul Democrat Frontul Salvarii Nationale*)

PDSR   Party of Social Democracy in Romania (*Partidul Democratiei Sociale din Romania*)

PER   Romanian Ecological Party (*Partidul Ecologist Roman*)

PF   Popular Front (*Frontul Popular*)

PL '93   Liberal Party '93 (*Partidul Liberal '93*)

PMR   Romanian Workers' Party (*Partidul Muncitoresc Roman*)

PNL   National Liberal Party (*Partidul National Liberal*)

PNT   National Peasants Party (*Partidul National Taranesc*)

PNTCD   National Peasants Party Christian Democratic (*Partidul National Taranesc Crestin Democrat*)

PRM   Greater Romania Party (*Partidul Romania Mare*)

PSDR   Romanian Social Democratic Party (*Partidul Social Democrat Roman*)

PSM   Socialist Labor Party (*Partidul Socialist al Muncii*)

PUNR   Romanian National Unity (*Partidul Unitatii Nationale Romane*)

UDMR   Hungarian Democratic Union of Romania (*Uniunea Democrata Maghiara din Romania*)

USD   Social Democratic Union (*Uniunea Social Democrat*)

VR   A Future for Romania (*Viitor pentru Romania*)

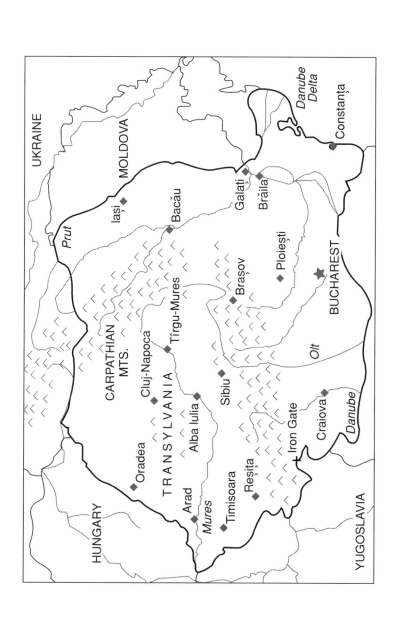

Map of Romania

Chapter 1

INTRODUCTION

The 1996 parliamentary and presidential elections were a turning
point in Romanian history. For the first time in almost sixty years,
voters used the ballot box to change the government. This "road to
normalcy" was marked by several twists and turns including a monar-
chical regime, an authoritarian government, almost forty-five years of
communist rule and the bloodiest of the 1989 Eastern European tran-
sitions.[1] While Romania might be on the road to normalcy, the challenges that the country faces are extraordinary. Like all East European
countries, Romania has had to undergo simultaneous political and
economic reform. However unlike the Visegrad countries of the Czech
Republic, Hungary and Poland, Romanian economic reform has been
lackluster. Moreover, there were always concerns regarding the level of
political reform and democracy during the presidency of Ion Iliescu.
Because of the lack of economic reform and the fragility of democracy,
Romania was excluded from the first round of NATO expansion and
EU[2] accession discussions, which had been the country's top foreign
policy priorities. Now as the country enters the 21st century, it has to
compete not only with its neighbors but also with the member-states of
the EU. The challenges facing Romania are formidable, but the opportunities are also immense. Romanian agriculture and chemical facilities
have great economic potential. The country's strategic geographic location makes it an important regional actor. The key question is whether
the government will pursue the economic policies necessary to transform the economy, provide stability to society and increase the
country's opportunity of joining Euro-Atlantic organizations.

In order to understand the current economic and political debates
occurring in the country, this book traces Romanian political and economic development since the creation of the new Romanian state in
the 19th century. Communist policies dominated the country's political
life from 1944 until 1989, and the legacies of communism still haunt it
today. Moreover, the nationalism of the Iron Guard during the 1940s
has much in common with the rhetoric of today's nationalist parties.
This is not to suggest that Romanian prewar and interwar history
have *predetermined* postcommunist politics.[3] However, the debates
that occur today over land reform, ethnic minority educational policy

and the role of the monarchy reflect some of the same debates that have occurred throughout the existence of the Romanian state. To understand the current debates, this section examines the issues that have historically shaped Romanian political development.

THE CREATION OF THE ROMANIAN STATE

Like their counterparts in Central Europe, the Romanian liberals of 1848 wanted to establish an ethnic state. At that time, Romanians inhabited a number of territories but were primarily concentrated in the principalities of Wallachia and Moldavia. These principalities were caught between the Ottoman and Russian empires. While liberal reform was never enacted in Moldavia, the Wallachian "forty-eighters" were able to briefly establish a provisional government that promised political and economic reform.[4] Russian intervention eliminated any opportunity for Romanian self-government, but in 1859 the Moldavian and Wallachian principalities each elected Alexandru Ioan Cuza as prince, thereby creating a *de facto* union between the two. Cuza's reign only lasted eight years before he was deposed and replaced by Prince Carol I of the German Hohenzollern-Sigmaringer dynasty. Following the Berlin Congress, the principalities achieved independence in 1878 and were recognized as a kingdom in 1881.

While many Romanians lived in the Old Kingdom, approximately four million Romanians lived in the surrounding territories of Bessarabia, Bukovina and Transylvania.[5] They were completely alienated from the ruling elite and subject to policies of ethnic assimilation. Several politicians in the Old Kingdom, most notably Premier Ion Bratianu, advocated the unification of the Old Kingdom with these territories. By the end of World War I, as the Austro-Hungarian empire collapsed, ethnic Romanians in these territories declared a union with the Old Kingdom.[6] By 1919, the territory and population of Greater Romania had more than doubled; however, ethnic Romanians comprised only half of the population in these newly acquired territories.

THE INTERWAR PERIOD

The period between 1918 and 1940 produced profound changes in the development of the Romanian nation and state. Emerging from World War I in 1918, Greater Romania was much larger, more populated and much more ethnically diverse than the old state. However by 1940, the country had lost much of this territory under the terms of the Second Vienna Award and the Molotov-Ribbentrop Pact. Northern Transylvania, Northern Bukovina and all of Bessarabia were quickly incorporated into other states. For Romania, the interwar period was one of territory and populations won and lost and democracy promised and destroyed. The beginning of the period, however, held great potential for the country.

During the 1920s, Romanian politics were generally more stable and more democratic than at any other point during the interwar period. While there were nine different governments, most of them were led by either the National Peasants Party (*Partidul National Taranesc* or PNT) or the National Liberal Party (*Partidul National Liberal* or PNL).[7] In addition, the monarchy under King Ferdinand provided stability to the political process. This was essential because under the 1923 constitution, the king had the power to appoint and to dismiss cabinet ministers as well as to veto legislation and to issue discretionary regulations. The issues that dominated the legislative agenda of the 1920s included land reform, industrialization and cultural policies.

During this period, the government implemented educational and linguistic reforms in the new territories to forge a new Romanian urban elite. These policies were intended to assimilate certain ethnic groups (such as the Szeklers in Transylvania and the Germans in Bukovina) and differentiate other ethnic groups (Jews throughout all of the newly incorporated territories and Hungarians in Transylvania). These policies were designed to create a new Romanian nation; however, the nationalism advocated by the state engendered extremist reactions from several groups, particularly students. Irina Livezeanu argues that "[y]outhful radical nationalists became the most committed freelance nation builders."[8] Student leaders of Romania's "new generation" of the 1920s believed that the state's nation-building policies needed to go much further in developing the nation.

The nationalism of the 1920s attempted to isolate ethnic Hungarians and Jews, and these ethnic groups had difficulty assimilating into the political process and into the traditional parties such as the PNT and the PNL. Instead, they created their own parties and many turned increasingly towards the Romanian Communist Party (*Partidul Comunist Roman* or PCR). The PCR was founded in May

1921. Before 1921, the communists had operated within the Romanian Social Democratic Party (*Partidul Social Democrat Roman* or PSDR).[9] While several nationalist organizations increased their membership in the 1920s, the PCR's membership was extremely low, often numbering in the hundreds. There were a number of reasons why the PCR was so unpopular. Firstly, it was a member of the Communist International (Comintern), and the Soviets placed their own foreign policy goals above the PCR's need to become a legitimate political force. For example, the PCR supported the position that Bessarabia should be relinquished to the Soviet Union. This made it very unpopular with the population. To many, particularly farmers, the PCR was considered antinationalist. Secondly, the party's ideology of class conflict was not suited to the conditions of the country. Romania was overwhelmingly an agricultural country, and there was no aggressive industrialization program that would have developed a class-consciousness. Finally, the PCR was viewed as a foreign organization. It was largely composed of ethnic Hungarians and Jews. In fact, ethnic Romanians constituted less than 25% of the membership, and ethnic Hungarians and Jews held many of the party's leading positions.[10]

In 1924, the ruling PNL outlawed the PCR, and the Soviets and the PCR leadership hoped to use this event as propaganda to attract more members; however, the PCR was too distrusted by the population. Therefore during the 1920s, the party exerted little influence on electoral outcomes or policy decisions. The party was fighting two battles. Firstly, it was coming under constant criticism from the Soviet Union for its lack of organization and political success. The PCR had to adjust its policies to appease the Soviet Union. Secondly, it had to prove to the Romanian population that it was not a tool of the Soviets. With these two conflicting objectives, it is easy to understand why the party lacked any political influence during this period.[11]

The conflicts between the PCR and the Comintern lasted until 1931. At the Fifth Congress of the Comintern the differences between the party and the Soviet leadership were settled. These problems were of course resolved in a manner most beneficial to the Soviet Union and its foreign policy objectives. The PCR's ideological and organizational bases were strictly established along Soviet lines.[12] This move ensured that for the next decade, the party would not be a political force; consequently, when the PCR came to power in the mid-1940s, it had to rely on the Soviet Union for legitimacy.

THE 1930s AND THE DEVELOPMENT OF THE PCR

One problem that plagued the PCR even after the Fifth Congress was the lack of consistent party leadership. During the interwar years, a number of Romanian communists were either imprisoned in Romania (home communists) or living in the Soviet Union (Muscovite communists). This left only a small group of Romanian communists free during the 1930s and the 1940s. This group consisted of men such as Stefan Foris and Lucretiu Patrascanu, who never developed any effective underground and were distrusted by both the home and Muscovite communists. There was not a unified leadership in the PCR; in fact, during this period, there was a clear division in the party's leadership. The dispute between the home and Muscovite communists was a general feature of Eastern European communist politics. The Soviet Union used this lack of party cohesion to increase its own policy options.

During the 1930s, Gheorghe Gheorghiu-Dej was one of the symbols of Romanian communism. His initial claim to fame was organizing the 1933 railway workshop strikes in the city of Grivita. Though he was actually arrested before the strike, Gheorghiu-Dej was considered its architect, and he was one of the few popular PCR figures. He was sent to jail in 1933 and remained there until 1944. Although he was imprisoned, Gheorghiu-Dej was still active in the party's leadership. The home communists recognized him as the party's leader while in jail, and the Muscovite group endorsed Gheorghiu-Dej's position because it felt that they could use him as their puppet.[13]

Those men who were imprisoned with Gheorghiu-Dej would later form the core of the party's leadership and included Gheorghe Apostol, Chivu Stoica, Alexandru Moghioros and Nicolae Ceausescu. Those home communists who were not imprisoned with Gheorghiu-Dej, such as Patrascanu, automatically became suspect. Gheorghiu-Dej's elevation to party secretary while in jail demonstrates how desperate the PCR and the Soviets were for a popular figure. The party hoped that he would become the popular symbol that it did not have during the 1920s. Because of his working-class background, it was assumed that he would be able to form associations with workers. He was also an ethnic Romanian, and this was particularly important because the Muscovite communists were mostly Jewish and ethnic Hungarians who were distrusted by the population. While the PCR failed to attract a significant following, several right-wing organizations enjoyed popularity, particularly with youths.

THE MONARCHY AND THE RISE OF THE RIGHT-WING

The 1930s in Romania has been described as the period of the "ebbing of democracy."[14] Democratic institutions such as the parliament, lost or ceded power to the monarchy. Unlike his father Ferdinand, King Carol II did not support parliamentary democracy or the traditional parties. At the same time that parliamentary democracy was weakening, right-wing nationalism was intensifying. University students in the Moldavian provincial capital of Iasi in the 1920s assisted in the formation of the League of National Christian Defense. With the guidance of the well-known anti-Semite A. C. Cuza, the dean of the University of Iasi Law School, students began to harass Jewish students and threaten Jewish newspaper editors. Students were organized under the leadership of Corneliu Zelea Codreanu, a law school student and strident nationalist, and in 1927 he organized the Legion of Archangel Michael (*Legiunea Arhanghelului Mihail* or LAM).[15]

By the early 1930s, the LAM had organized a political unit called the Iron Guard. The traditional parties banned the Iron Guard, but it continued its political activity under the newly created All for the Country party. Although Carol and the traditional parties opposed the fascist ideology of the Iron Guard, they felt that they could use it for their own political purposes. During the 1937 parliamentary election, Iuliu Maniu, leader of the PNT, signed an electoral pact with Codreanu. This agreement brought some measure of respect to the Iron Guard. As a consequence through its party affiliation, the Iron Guard received almost 16% of the vote.[16] The election was also significant because for the first time in an election, the party that organized the election was unable to form the government. While the PNL received a plurality of the vote, Carol asked Octavian Goga, a respected poet and leader of the right-wing National Christian Party, to form the government. The coalition government lasted only two months before Carol abolished the 1923 constitution and replaced it with another that gave him broad powers. In March, he banned all parties and began to take action against the Iron Guard. Members of the Iron Guard and the PCR were jailed and in November 1938, Codreanu was killed.[17] Carol's attempt at ruling, however, was less than successful, and by 1939 he had begun to work with the traditional parties and even the Iron Guard.

INTERWAR FOREIGN POLICY

Romanian foreign policy during the interwar period attempted to maintain the Versailles system that had established the boundaries of

Greater Romania. The country cultivated relations with France and, to a lesser extent, Great Britain as a means of ensuring its territorial integrity. Because of the acquisition of Bessarabia and the PCR's activity, Romania had poor relations with the Soviet Union. Similarly, because of border disputes, foreign policy with Hungary and Bulgaria was hindered. While the country wanted to preserve the Versailles system, German conquests in Europe and concerns about the Soviet Union and Hungary forced Carol to cultivate relations with Hitler while the Nazis developed relations with the Iron Guard and leaders of Romania's right-wing.

During 1938 and 1939, Romania forged closer economic relations with Germany while attempting to remain neutral. Romanian oil and agricultural products were viewed by the Nazis as essential for their mounting war effort. The signing of the nonaggression pact between Germany and the Soviet Union on 23 August 1939 and the success of the German campaigns in 1940 forced Carol to abandon neutrality and fully cooperate with Germany. Carol hoped that the Germans would guarantee the territorial integrity of Romania and ensure that Bessarabia would not be returned to the Soviet Union.

However, he did not know that as part of the nonaggression pact, Soviet Foreign Minister Molotov and German Foreign Minister Ribbentrop had agreed to the annexation of Bessarabia and Northern Bukovina by the Soviet Union. The Romanian government was finally notified of this agreement on 26 June 1940. Carol attempted to negotiate with the Soviets, but Molotov refused to re-examine the issue. He then appealed to Germany for assistance, but German officials stationed in Bucharest indicated that the agreement was based on Hitler's orders.[18] Carol and his advisors had no alternative but to yield to Soviet demands. On 28 June, Soviet forces quickly began to occupy the territories. By 3 July, all of Bessarabia and Northern Bukovina were under Soviet control.[19] Carol's attention was now focused on ensuring that other territories were not annexed by Hungary and Bulgaria.

Realizing the need to forge even closer relations, Carol appointed a cabinet that was much more pro-German, including members of the Iron Guard. However, Hitler's need for support in Hungary and Bulgaria was more important than Romanian domestic politics. In September 1940, Romania was pressured to sign the Treaty of Craiova with Bulgaria which relinquished Romania's territory of Southern Dobrudja to Bulgaria. Negotiations with Hungary over the status of

Transylvania were much more contentious. Hitler decided to award a large portion of Transylvania to Hungary but guarantee Romania's new borders. While many Romanian politicians urged Carol to reject Hitler's offer, he decided that he had no alternative but to accept. On 30 August 1940, the cessation of Transylvania was formally announced, by which time Romania had lost 30% of her territory and population.[20]

THE ASCENSION OF THE IRON GUARD

After relinquishing Transylvania, public opinion turned against the King. Marshall Ion Antonescu, who had earlier served as minister of defense, was asked by Carol in September to form a new government. Antonescu initially had close relations with the Iron Guard and was an acceptable candidate to Germany. Carol issued a decree that provided Antonescu unlimited power. Antonescu, who had a great disdain for the King, negotiated with the leaders of the PNT and the PNL to form a government. These leaders made any government formation conditional on the removal of Carol. Antonescu finally presented him an ultimatum: Either abdicate in favor of his nineteen-year-old son Michael or face the possibility forced removal. Carol quickly renounced the throne and left the country.

On 6 September, Michael assumed the throne and signed a decree granting Antonescu full powers. Antonescu quickly moved to establish his authority and his relationship with Germany. While he established close relations with Germany, his relationship with the Iron Guard deteriorated. He began to view the leaders of the Iron Guard as incompetent and dangerous. Finally with the backing of Berlin, Antonescu purged members of the Iron Guard from his cabinet. By January 1941, he had established a military dictatorship.[21] In June, Romania joined Germany in a declaration of war against the Soviet Union. Throughout the war, Antonescu maintained his alliance with Germany; however, he realized after the German defeat at Stalingrad that the Soviet Union was now in a much stronger position. Between 1941 and 1944, Maniu and other party leaders made overtures to the Allies to prevent the advancing Soviet military from capturing the country. Because of the fear of a Soviet occupation, Antonescu treated the PCR very harshly. By 1944, he had alienated several parties and the monarchy, and these parties and King Michael instigated a coup against him in August 1944. While the role of the PCR in the coup was relatively minor, with the aid of the Soviet army it emerged as the dominant party by the late 1940s.

This book traces the development of the Romanian communist and postcommunist transition. In order to understand these periods, it is instructive to examine the personal politics of Gheorghiu-Dej and Ceausescu. While these two men had many differences, Ceausescu inherited a regime from Gheorghiu-Dej that provided him some level of autonomy from the Soviet Union and ultimately complete control of the party, state and society. Chapter 2 examines the origins of Romanian communist leadership and the development of the Gheorghiu-Dej regime. In 1944 the PCR was completely dependent on the Soviet Union for its legitimacy; however by 1964, Romanian foreign and economic policy diverged from Soviet dictates. Chapter 3 discusses how Ceausescu manipulated the personal politics of Romanian communism to create his own personality cult. He followed Gheorghiu-Dej's policies of industrialization and autonomy to create one of the most isolated Eastern European regimes. As a consequence of his failed economic policies, persecution of ethnic minorities and inability to establish any real legitimacy, Ceausescu sowed the seeds for the 1989 revolution.

Chapter 4 explores how Ceausescu's legacy influenced the institutional and party development of postcommunist Romania. Because of this legacy, Romanian political development since 1990 has been different from other East European countries. Chapter 5 analyzes the country's economic policies since 1990. While Romania began the decade with many economic advantages, the inability to privatize and implement monetary reform has had a devastating effect on the economy. Chapter 6 discusses the country's foreign policy since 1990 and explores efforts at Euro-Atlantic integration. While Romania has always had a Western-oriented foreign policy, the lack of democratization and economic reform has limited the country's opportunities. The status of Romania's ethnic minorities, particularly ethnic Hungarians, has been an important foreign policy issue, and membership of organizations such as the Council of Europe has been based on the treatment of ethnic minorities.

Romania's unfinished revolution involves five issues: political legitimacy, civil society, Western acceptance, ethnic relations and economic development. These issues were considered by many to be the goals of the revolution. However, they have not been fulfilled. The violence associated with the miners' strikes of 1990, 1991 and 1999 demonstrate a lack of political legitimacy among Romanian politicians and institutions. This lack of political legitimacy affects the development of Romanian civil society. Communist leadership had suppressed the creation of civil society. Unlike other Eastern European countries in 1989, Romania did not have a developed opposition movement. The revolution was supposed to inject political participation into the country's politics. However as the miners' strikes demonstrate, violence is still the preferred means of political expression among certain segments of the society.

While Romania is a member of the Council of Europe and several other Western institutions, the country was not included in the first wave of NATO expansion nor EU discussions on full membership. Romania has not gained the acceptance by Western institutions that other East European countries enjoy. The inclusion of an ethnic Hungarian organization in the government in 1996 was suppose to demonstrate that the country's ethnic relations had improved. However, disputes over an ethnic Hungarian-language university and the rise of nationalist parties demonstrate that this goal of the revolution has not been attained. Finally, the revolution was suppose to eliminate the economic hardships that Romanians endured during the 1980s, but instead economic conditions for many have not improved. While some enjoy a higher standard of living, the standard for many segments of population, especially the elderly, has worsened. The Romanian revolution occurred in 1989, but it may take decades to complete.

1 Michael Shafir, "Romania's Road to 'Normalcy,'" *Journal of Democracy*, April 1997, pp. 144–158.

2 Throughout the book, I use the term European Union or EU, though technically the European Economic Community (EEC) was not renamed the EU until the signing of the Maastricht Treaty in December 1991.

3 For a discussion of path dependency see, Margaret Levi, "A Model, a Method, and a Map: Rational Choice in Comparative and Historical Analysis," in Mark Irving Lichbach and Alan S. Zuckerman, eds., *Comparative Politics: Rationality, Culture, and Structure* (Cambridge: Cambridge University Press, 1997), pp. 28–29.

4 Keith Hitchens, *Romania 1866-1947* (Oxford: Clarendon Press, 1994), pp. 1–10.

5 Ibid, p. 202.

6 For a more complete analysis of the union of Bessarabia with the Old Kingdom see, Dumitru Almas and Ioan Scurtu, "Unirea Basarabiei cu Romania: Confirmarea internationala a acestui act istoric," in Ioan Scurtu, et. al., eds., *Istoria Basarabiei de la inceputuri pana in 1998* (Bucharest: Editura Semne, 1998), pp. 80–89.

7 Stelian Neagoe, *Istoria Guvernelor Romaniei* (Bucharest: Editura Machiavelli, 1995).

8 Irina Livezeanu, *Cultural Politics in Greater Romania: Regionalism, Nation Building, and Ethnic Struggle, 1918-1930* (Ithaca, NY: Cornell University Press, 1995), p. 301.

9   For a discussion concerning the split between the PSDR and the PCR see, Nicolae Jurca, *Social democratia in Romania* (Sibiu: Editura Hermann, 1993), pp. 9–36.

10 Michael Shafir, *Romania: Politics, Economics and Society* (Boulder, CO: Lynne Reinner Publishers, 1985), p. 26.

11 For an excellent account of the development of the PCR see, Robert R. King, *History of the Romanian Communist Party* (Stanford: Hoover Institution Press, 1980).

12 Ioan Scurtu, *Viata politica din Romania: 1918–1944* (Bucharest: Editura Albatros, 1982), pp. 135–136.

13 Muscovite leader Ana Pauker had earlier been in a Romanian jail until a prisoner exchange in 1940 sent her to the Soviet Union.

14 Hitchens, *Romania 1866-1947*, p. 416.

15 For a complete history of the development of university student fascism see, Livezeanu, *Cultural Politics in Greater Romania: Regionalism, Nation Building, and Ethnic Struggle, 1918–1930*, pp. 211–296.

16 C. Enescu, "Semnificatia alegerilor din decembrie 1937 in evolutia politica a neamului romanesc," in Petre Datculescu and Klaus Liepelt, eds., *Renaterea unei democratii alegerile din Romania de la 20 mai 1990* (Bucharest: IRSOP, 1991), pp. 145–175.

17 Ioan Scurtu, *Viata politica din Romania: 1918-1944*, pp. 199–201.

18 Ioan Scurtu and Constantin Hlihor, *Complot impotriva Romaniei* (Bucharest: Editura Academiei de Inalte Studii Militare, 1994).

19 Ioan Scurtu, Gheorghe I. Ionita and Stefania Dinu, "Ocuparea Basarabiei de catre Armata Rosie. Statutul Basarabiei in cadrul Uniunii Sovietice," in Ioan Scurtu, ed., *Istoria Basarabiei de la inceputuri pana in 1998* (Bucharest: Editura Semne, 1998), pp. 202–227.

20 Mihail Manoilescu, *Distatul de la Viena: Memorii iulie-august 1940* (Bucharest: Editura Enciclopedica, 1991).

21 Hitchens argues that the Antonescu government was a military dictatorship rather than a fascist regime because the government had no ideological basis. See, Hitchens, *Romania 1866–1947*, p. 469.

Chapter 2

By the late 1940s Romania, like most other Eastern European countries, was under Soviet influence and proclaimed itself a socialist country. However by the 1960s, the country had secured some autonomy from the Soviet Union and developed its own form of national communism. This was a crucial period for the development of Romanian communism. Gheorghiu-Dej was a home communist, and Stalin distrusted these communists. While other home communists were purged in the 1940s, Gheorghiu-Dej consolidated his party power. He was a devout Stalinist, yet events in the 1950s such as Khrushchev's New Course and "secret speech" ushered in new regimes throughout Eastern Europe. While other regimes were purged because of their ties to Stalin, Gheorghiu-Dej maintained his party position. In the 1960s, the Soviet Union, Czechoslovakia, East Germany and Poland urged the economic integration of Eastern Europe. This meant that a country such as Romania would be primarily responsible for exporting foodstuffs and agricultural products, but Gheorghiu-Dej resisted any attempts to limit the country's industrialization policies. This chapter explores how Gheorghiu-Dej maintained his power while other Eastern European leaders were replaced, and how the nation-building of the 1920s and the 1930s affected communist nation-building in the 1950s. This chapter analyzes these questions and places Romanian political development within a larger Eastern European context.

THE AUGUST 1944 COUP

The years between 1944 and 1947 witnessed a great upheaval in Romanian politics. The PCR developed from a minor party to actually assuming political control, and the division between the home and Muscovite communists grew during these years. In the case of Romania, these groups had conflicting views regarding the importance of the August 1944 coup and the composition of the country's initial popular front governments. The coup of 23 August 1944 was a crucial event in the development of the PCR's mythology. Gheorghiu-Dej and his supporters claimed that they conceived of the coup while in prison. The home communists viewed this issue as vital to their political future, and they felt that their direct association with the coup would help them consolidate their relationship with the people.

By 1944, the Romanian opposition led by Maniu was negotiating an armistice with the Allies that would provide for the immediate surrender of Romania on the condition that the Allies would assure the country's independence and territorial integrity. The opposition's desire to end the war led to the creation of the Patriotic Front. This organization was composed of the PNT, the PNL, the PSDR and the PCR. The united opposition stated that it would overthrow the Antonescu regime and support the Allied war effort if their conditions were met. However, none of the Allies were willing to grant all of the conditions. Antonescu continued to support Germany, and while he probably knew that the war was lost, he was concerned about the advancing Soviet army as well as the possibility of a German-led coup. Antonescu's support of Hitler was probably because he "saw no other viable alternative."[1]

Antonescu and the opposition were concerned that the Soviets would use the war effort as an excuse to enter Romania and take over the country. These concerns were well grounded because while the opposition continued negotiating for the country's withdrawal, the Allies had already agreed that Romania would belong to the Soviet sphere of influence. On 20 August 1944, the Soviet army crossed the Romanian border. The swiftness of the Soviet advance caught the opposition by surprise and so they quickly decided to organize the coup for 23 August. On the day of the coup, Antonescu met with King Michael who urged him to accept an immediate armistice. When Antonescu refused, the King had him and his associates arrested. Gheorghiu-Dej later claimed that he and the PCR conceived of the coup and that the other parties, as well as King Michael, agreed to overthrow Antonescu only when it became clear that the Soviets would overrun the country.[2] While the communists played a less significant role in the coup, they did take custody of Antonescu soon after his arrest.

Aside from the coup, the significant issue at this time was the internal struggle raging between the home and Muscovite communists. Gheorghiu-Dej led the home communists during the interwar period while Ana Pauker and Vasile Luca led the Muscovite communists. Months before the coup, Pauker and Luca were in the Soviet Union planning their route to power. They argued that the existing government structures should be eliminated when they and the Soviet army entered Romania. They maintained that the role of the Romanian communists, meaning home communists, should be to assist them and the army and engage in no independent actions. The Pauker group believed that it would be the Soviet army that would "liberate" the country. Pauker's concern was focused on increasing the ranks of the party and assisting the Soviets in fighting the Germans. For example, the Muscovite communists were responsible for the creation of the Tudor Vladimirescu brigade. This military unit was composed of Romanian prisoners of war, and its purpose was to provide armed support for the Soviet army. This group would eventually form the backbone of the Romanian secret police.

The home communists felt that by actively assisting the coup, they might garner some measure of popular support for the PCR. They believed that to supplant the Muscovite communists, and gain the trust of the Soviet leadership, they would need the support of the population. The Soviet Union encouraged both of these groups to increase its policy alternatives. During this time, popular support was regarded by the Soviets as necessary to fight the Germans. Therefore in 1944, the Soviets' primary objective was toppling the Antonescu regime and mobilizing the population, rather than establishing a communist state apparatus. As with the Comintern, they placed their own foreign policy goals before the needs of the PCR. The Soviet Union encouraged the party to form alliances with the other parties of the Patriotic Front.

The Soviets knew that the PCR did not have a sufficiently broad base of support to form the government and that a coalition government was required. As a consequence, they needed Gheorghiu-Dej and Patrascanu, as well as other ethnic Romanians, in order to appeal to the population and other political forces. Because a coalition government was necessary, Gheorghiu-Dej was afforded the opportunity to demonstrate his loyalty to the Soviet Union. However during this time, the Pauker group still exerted a great deal of influence.[3] Because it was the coup that brought him to power, Gheorghiu-Dej placed a great deal of importance in the event. The coup's primary political effect was to provide home communists with government positions and to assist them in consolidating their power. Therefore, unlike the situation in most of the other Eastern European countries, the Soviet occupation benefited those who had not spent the interwar years in the Soviet Union.

THE EARLY POSTWAR GOVERNMENTS

Following the war in both East Germany and Poland, structural disintegration occurred so rapidly that the communist parties faced no real political competition. In these countries, the parties quickly established themselves in positions of power. In Romania, however, both the monarchy and government structures remained, and this partially accounts for the establishment of popular front governments. Between 1944 and 1948, the country had numerous governments with different political compositions. King Michael designated the first government following the coup, and it included representatives from all the major parties. General Constantin Sanatescu, one of the army commanders who assisted the Patriotic Front, was chosen prime minister. His cabinet included coup leaders such as Maniu (PNT), Dinu Bratianu (PNL), C. Titel Petrescu (PSDR) and Patrascanu (PCR). Even though the major parties were represented, certain parties received far more cabinet positions (e.g., the PCR). The Soviets exerted a great deal of influence in these post-coup governments, and portfolios were assigned based on political reliability.

The PCR formed coalition governments with these other parties for two reasons. Firstly in 1944, the Soviet Union and the PCR could not unilaterally decide Romania's fate. While Churchill had agreed that the Soviet Union would have 90% control over Romania and an armistice had been signed in 1944, the specifics of the peace agreement were not finalized until 1947. The Soviet Union and the PCR were restricted in their activity because of these negotiations, and therefore, cooperation with the PNT and PNL provided the coalition governments with greater legitimacy. The Soviet Union did not want to alarm either Great Britain or the United States by immediately imposing a communist regime. The Soviet Union and the PCR gradually consolidated their influence within the coalition governments. Secondly, the Soviet Union promoted these governments in order to provide the PCR with a measure of legitimacy. Certain organizations and parties were invited to participate in the formation of the governments in order to build the party's popular support.

Following the coup, the Soviets infiltrated the two most important institutions in Romania, the military and the secret police. The Soviets immediately redirected the Romanian military effort towards fighting the German forces in Hungary. In addition, the *siguranta* (the Romanian secret police) was taken over by the Soviets. Communists were placed in charge of the day-to-day operations of both the military and the *siguranta*. Therefore, while the Soviets in theory allowed for power sharing among the various parties, in reality the Soviets and the PCR controlled most of the sensitive military posts.

Due to internal pressures, the first Sanatescu government lasted only two months. In November 1944, a second Sanatescu government was formed that reflected the growing power of the PCR.[4] This government lasted less than a month due to internal fighting among the parties. The third government in as many months was created when King Michael designated General Nicolae Radescu as prime minister. General Radescu was not supported by the Soviets, and this move by King Michael demonstrated that they had not completely consolidated their power over all institutions. The Soviets were cautious because they did not want the Allies brought into a discussion concerning Romanian internal politics.

With each change in the government, the communists garnered more positions and influence. The litmus test that was used in choosing officials was the individual's desire to cooperate with the Soviet Union. In October 1944, the National Democratic Front was established. It included the PCR, the PSDR, the Union of Patriots and the Plowman's Front. These parties and fronts formed a coalition government with the PCR because they represented segments of society that the communists felt they would need future support from. The Union of Patriots was an amalgamation of intellectuals and professionals that really never had any political influence; however, the communists realized that these groups would be vital in building the economic and social infrastructure that they wanted. One important consequence of the struggle for power was that it promoted and protected Romanian nationalism. Because the traditional parties existed, nationalism was not totally eliminated.

THE GROZA GOVERNMENT AND THE PCR

The Plowman's Front was particularly popular in Transylvania in the 1930s, but by the 1940s it had become merely an extension of the PCR. The leader of the Plowman's Front was Petru Groza. He had participated in the governments of the 1920s and brought legitimacy to the National Democratic Front. King Michael was finally forced by the Soviets to dissolve the Radescu government, and in March 1945 the Groza government was installed.[5] Gheorghiu-Dej was given the influential post of minister of transportation, and Patrascanu was also made a prominent member of the Groza cabinet. The Soviet Union returned to Romania the administration of Northern Transylvania. During this time, the United States and Britain argued that the Groza government did not represent democratic forces, but by this time they exerted no influence on the country's development.

Immediately following the 1944 coup, the PCR engaged in a policy of rapid recruitment. The recruitment campaign targeted workers from various sectors and even Iron Guard members. The campaign became part of the debate between the home and Muscovite communists. They were competing for members, and each group wanted to increase the ranks of the PCR by increasing their own ranks. The more members a group could enlist, the greater their share of party power. It was Pauker who engineered the entrance of Iron Guard members (which was later used against her). The home communists were not in a position to object to Pauker's obvious stacking of the PCR's membership. Even though Gheorghiu-Dej was the party secretary, Muscovite communists still dominated the party's Politburo.

Aside from the division between home and Muscovite communists, there was also a division among the home communists. The Gheorghiu-Dej and Emil Bordnaras faction argued that Patrascanu had attempted to create a popular movement around himself. They accused him of using his influence in the government to usurp the party's power. While Patrascanu was an important figure in the early Romanian postwar governments, he was later purged from the party and executed.

In May 1945 the Sovroms (Soviet-Romanian joint-stock companies) were created. Sixteen Sovroms were established by the Soviets to exploit the vast natural resources of the country. In addition, the Soviets also exacted large reparation payments from Romania. Under the terms of the armistice, the Romanian government paid the Soviets US$300 million in the form of oil, timber, grain and other natural resources. This amount covered the damages that the country had inflicted on the Soviet Union during the war. Furthermore, the government paid for the stationing of Soviet troops that numbered almost 150,000 in 1946.[6] The total goods and services delivered to the Soviet Union from September 1944 through June 1948 was approximately US$2 billion. This amount was 86% of the country's total GNP, and this left the government and the PCR with little economic means. Therefore, both institutions were dependent on the Soviet Union for financial resources. Gheorghiu-Dej subsequently made economic development a primary focus of his leadership.

By 1947, the Groza government had abolished the PNT and the PNL. Soon afterwards, King Michael was forced to abdicate on 31 December 1947. By the late 1940s, Gheorghiu-Dej had held numerous positions in the Groza government, including minister of transportation, minister of the national economy and minister of industry. It was in his capacity as minister of the national economy that he won Moscow's support by executing its economic program.

INTERNATIONAL POLITICS AND CONFLICT IN THE PCR

By the early 1950s, the Romanian communists had no choice but to engage in the complete Stalinization of the country. Like their Muscovite counterparts, the home communists under Gheorghiu-Dej had no independent source of legitimacy; their power was almost completely derived from Soviet authority. Although Gheorghiu-Dej was the most popular PCR member, the popular front governments never provided the party with any real popular support. Throughout Eastern Europe, Stalinization advocated collectivization and industrialization. These policies became additional areas of competition between the home and Muscovite communists. They measured the success of Stalinization in terms of the political advantage that they gained. The basis of Stalinization was not so much social transformation as party transformation. Therefore, it is understandable why the collectivization and the industrialization policies of the 1940s and the 1950s failed.

The PCR, like other Eastern European parties, found that the population was vehemently opposed to collectivization. Pauker was primarily responsible for agricultural policy, and her fellow Muscovite communist Luca assisted her. The peasants' violent opposition to collectivization illustrated the legitimacy crisis of the communists. Between 1949 and 1950, hundreds of collectivization teams were turned away by the peasants who refused to allow their land to be expropriated. However, the peasants were eventually forcibly collectivized.

Collectivization was not the major priority of the PCR's Stalinization program, but party members were concerned about the political consequences of not implementing collectivization. Therefore, they engaged in a blatant campaign of misinformation to hide their lack of success. The Romanian leadership reported to the Soviet Union that during 1950, 1,029 collective farms had been established. In reality by 1950, there were only 56 collective farms in the country.[7]

The home communists blamed the failed agricultural policies on Pauker and Luca, exploiting the collectivization policy on two fronts. Firstly, they blamed the violence of collectivization on the Muscovites. Gheorghiu-Dej argued that the home communists had put forward the principle of voluntary participation in collectivization. He maintained that the Pauker group had disregarded this principle. He received popular support for condemning the violence of this campaign, but of course he never mentioned that he had been a supporter of Pauker's methods of collectivization.

Secondly, Gheorghiu-Dej and the other home communists wanted to distance themselves from the Pauker group to avoid any of the political fallout that might accompany the failure of collectivization. The Soviets were not pleased with either the progress of Romanian collectivization or with the distorted statistics that they were given. With the blame squarely on the shoulders of the Pauker group, the home communists would gain a political advantage with the Soviet leadership.

Industrial expansion was the priority of the PCR and the home communists. Eventually, Gheorghiu-Dej became convinced that rapid industrialization would provide the party with economic autonomy that would translate into political autonomy. Heavy industrialization was stressed while other projects, namely collectivization, were de-emphasized. Although he pursued a policy of industrialization because of Soviet dictates, Gheorghiu-Dej also supported industrialization because he felt that it could assist him in consolidating his own political power. Although he was emerging as the *de facto* leader of Romania, Gheorghiu-Dej encountered a tremendous amount of opposition from the Muscovite communists. In July of 1948 the government established the State Planning Commission which was responsible for submitting reports to the government on the country's general economic condition, formulating a general plan for the national economy (central planning) and executing economic planning. The first chairman of the State Planning Commission was Gheorghiu-Dej, and he used the position to demonstrate that he was a loyal Stalinist by instituting Soviet central planning.

THE VERIFICATION CAMPAIGN

By the 1950s, the PCR and the PSDR had merged to form the Romanian Workers' Party (*Partidul Muncitoresc Roman* or PMR). The party engaged in two campaigns to eliminate opposition. The first campaign, which lasted from March 1945 through December 1947, destroyed traditional political forces. The second campaign started in 1946 and was designed to purge and consolidate the PMR. Although the party did not have broad popular support, individuals joined the PMR for the political and financial benefits that it offered. In addition, the party had grown substantially because of the absorption of the PSDR and Iron Guard members. The verification campaign reassessed the credentials of members from these groups. By May 1950, the verification campaign had concluded, and approximately 340,000 members had been eliminated from the party. By the mid-1950s, party membership had dropped approximately 20% to less than 600,000.[8] Between 1948 and 1955, some 450,000 members were expelled from the party (see Table 2.1). This drastic reduction in overall party membership was accompanied by an increase in the membership of select groups. The verification campaign was aimed not only at eliminating "bourgeois" elements from the party but at increasing the proportion of certain socioeconomic groups such as workers.

The verification campaign was not immune to the conflict between the home and Muscovite communists. The campaign was viewed by both groups as an opportunity to increase their power in the party. Many of the individuals whom the Pauker group had brought in after the August coup were targeted by the home communists as unacceptable. This was especially true of the Iron Guard members that Pauker

TABLE 2.1   COMMUNIST PARTY MEMBERSHIP: 1944–1964

DATE	NUMBER OF PARTY MEMBERS
Before August 1944	884
February 1945	16,000
March 1945	35,000
April 1945	42,633
June/July 1945	101,810
October 1945	256,863
June 1946	717,490
January 1947	704,857
September 1947	720,000
December 1947	803,831
February 1948	1,060,000
May 1950	720,000
December 1955	595,398
June 1958	720,000
June 1960	834,600
December 1961	900,000
December 1964	1,377,847

Source: Robert King, *A History of the Romanian Communist Party*, (Stanford, CA: Hoover Institution Press, 1980), p. 64.

had personally brought into the party. By the end of the verification campaign, the home communists had been quite successful in eliminating Muscovite supporters from the party and thereby increasing their power. The campaign of 1948 was a precursor of the 1952 purges.

In addition to the verification campaign itself, the new party statutes regarding membership certainly favored the home communists. The emphasis on admitting working-class members benefited the home communists, due in large part to Gheorghiu-Dej's image. He was still remembered for the railway strike in Grivita some fifteen years earlier. This segment of society associated itself much more with him than with Pauker. Therefore the home communists were assured that most of the new party recruits would not become aligned with the Muscovites.

The outcome of the verification campaign demonstrated that the home communists had Stalin's support to change party statutes, but why did Stalin allow them to increase their power? Following the 1944 coup, the Muscovite communists were certainly in a stronger position than the home communists. They had greater support from the Soviet Union and were more organized. Moreover, in other Eastern European countries, Stalin had actively supported the Muscovites. The decline of Romania's Muscovite communists was because of shifting Soviet alliances in the PMR. Stalin realized that initially the party, as well as the government, needed popular support. As a consequence he forged closer ties with the home communists because they were more acceptable to the population than the Muscovites. In addition, Stalin supported Gheorghiu-Dej because he was pleased by the manner in which Gheorghiu-Dej handled the reparation payments and Sovrom deliveries. Since they had no independent power base, the Muscovites' fortunes were dependent on the Soviet leadership. When the Soviets began to support the home communists, the Muscovites had no alternative but to accept their decision.

The verification campaign is only one example of how Gheorghiu-Dej consolidated his power in the party. He also used the ballot box to unify his power in the country and increase his own personal popularity among the people. In March 1951, national elections were held for all leading party organs. The Gheorghiu-Dej faction argued that the goal of these elections should be the "Romanianization" of the party (i.e., all Jewish and non-ethnic Romanians should be excluded from the party hierarchy). Gheorghiu-Dej maintained that the best candidates for party positions were those who had a working-class background and demonstrated loyalty to the party (using himself as an example).

He also emphasized the election of state workers to party posts. He was successful in having workers, technicians and army officers elected to party organs.[9] He stressed the election of state workers because Pauker's group held positions in the party apparatus. By placing his own people in the lower party organs, Gheorghiu-Dej successfully severed Pauker's hold over the party's grassroots. Although he had successfully consolidated his power, the Muscovite communists were still active in party politics. They still represented a potential threat, and as long as the Pauker group remained, there was the possibility that the Soviets could decide to support the Muscovites. Therefore from his perspective, the 1952 purges were important because they eliminated the only real alternative to his leadership.

THE 1952 PURGES

Within an Eastern European context, the Romanian party purges of the 1950s were an anomaly. Other Eastern European parties were purged in the early 1950s, but these parties purged the home not the Muscovite communists. Elsewhere the Muscovite communists were viewed as politically and personally closer to the Soviet Union. The home communists were viewed as potentially nationalistic and less politically reliable, but this was not the case in Romania. The 1952 purges can also be viewed in a strictly Romanian political context. These purges marked an important stage in Gheorghiu-Dej's consolidation of power and also dramatically increased party cohesion.

The purge of the Pauker group occurred swiftly. At a Central Committee plenum in February 1952, fraud was supposedly discovered in the currency reform program. The fraud was linked to the Ministry of Finance under the control of Luca. The Central Committee asked him to apologize for poorly implementing the currency reform. Luca readily agreed and issued a written apology. At this very same meeting, Pauker was charged with attempting to cover up the fraud, and she was accused of interfering with the Central Committee's investigation. The currency reform investigation became the pretext used by the home communists to purge the Pauker group.

In March, a commission convened, and Luca retracted his apology and denied the accusations. At this meeting he was supported by Pauker because she realized that the purge had begun, and they had to fight the allegations.[10] The accusations of corruption did not end with them. The Central Committee turned its attention to their party supporters. Luca's associates in the Ministry of Finance, the Foreign Trade Office and the State Bank were dismissed from their positions. The list of charges against Luca also expanded. During this time, Pauker was being isolated by the party. She was criticized for supporting Luca and was refused re-election to the Politburo and the Secretariat.

The purges did not end with the Central Committee meeting but continued throughout 1952. In June, Gheorghiu-Dej accused Pauker and Luca of hindering the collectivization and the industrialization programs. Finally in 1954, Luca was tried and sentenced to death, but his sentence was commuted to life imprisonment. Pauker was relieved of her party and government posts and placed under house arrest and died in 1960. Gheorghiu-Dej was the major beneficiary of the purges. In June 1952, he was appointed president of the Council of Ministers (premier). He combined this position with his post of party first secretary (which he had held since October 1945).

While the purges had far-reaching political ramifications, they had four immediate impacts. Firstly, they insulated the party, and more importantly Gheorghiu-Dej, from the blame that was associated with the failure of the Romanian economy. He and his party cohorts could blame the Pauker group for the economy's poor performance. The Muscovite communists were a convenient target since Pauker had been in charge of the collectivization program, and Luca had played an important role in both currency reform and industrialization. He used the purges to absolve himself and his group of any blame for the failed economy.

Gheorghiu-Dej had to be careful when criticizing the Pauker group. He had to guard against the possibility that some might interpret the purges as an attack on the party itself. The people had already associated the failed economic policies with the party. Gheorghiu-Dej had to not only distance himself from the Pauker group, but he also had to distance the Pauker group from the party. Therefore he argued that the Muscovite communists acted independently of the party. In an argument that he would use a decade later, he claimed that the party had opposed the economic policies of the Pauker group but that the Muscovites had supplanted the party's power.

Secondly, the purges persuaded other party factions to join the home communists. No faction wanted to be associated with the Muscovites, and the purges increased party cohesion. Michael Shafir argues that this cohesion was due, in large part, to what he terms "factional-anxiety."[11] He states that one of the central life experiences of Romanian party members, regardless of group orientation, was the endless factional strife in the party since its founding. The weak organizational structure of the party and the manipulation by the Soviets created an environment conducive to factionalization. The very survival of the party, and party members, became the focus of the party. Common life experiences solidified the Gheorghiu-Dej regime. Most of the party's hierarchy was imprisoned with Gheorghiu-Dej during the interwar period, and a bond developed between these individuals. His fellow prisoners such as Stoica, Apostol and Ceausescu rose to important positions in the party. Most of the home communists were in Romanian jails while Muscovite communists were in the Soviet Union.

Thirdly, the purges allowed the home communists to increase their influence in the party's organs. By May 1952, the composition of both the Secretariat and the Politburo contained a majority of home communists.[12] The fourth impact of the purges related to the level of Soviet influence in the party. Party members inferred that Gheorghiu-Dej had the backing of the Soviets. The party members reasoned that the purges, and Gheorghiu-Dej's consolidation of power, could have occurred only with the support of the Soviet Union. Therefore party members who opposed him would be opposing the Soviet Union. Although Soviet influence increased party cohesion in the PMR, the 1952 purges also chipped away at Soviet power in the party. Unlike the Muscovite communists, Gheorghiu-Dej did have some personal popularity. In addition, he had placed his own supporters in important government as well as party positions. He indirectly controlled various political, economic and social institutions. As Romania's leader, Gheorghiu-Dej still derived his authority and legitimacy from the Soviets, but he was also developing authority that was not dependent on the Soviet Union. This authority and party support would provide the regime some level of autonomy from the Soviet Union by the 1960s.

The Soviets allowed him to purge the Muscovite communists for two reasons. Firstly, Stalin had developed a close relationship with Gheorghiu-Dej that he did not have with other home communists. Gheorghiu-Dej had been responsible for delivering economic resources to Moscow and had embraced the policies of Stalinization. He wanted to transform the country from an agrarian society into a highly industrialized state. In many respects, he was not a typical Eastern European home communist. Stalin feared home communists because of their mass appeal. Home communists derived popular support for two basic reasons, either because of the popularity of the party or because of their own personal attributes. While Gheorghiu-Dej was popular among a segment of the population, his party had little genuine public support. His own personal popularity was kept in check by the party's image as a foreign movement. He did not have the popular support that home communists in other Eastern European countries enjoyed, and Stalin knew that he did not pose a serious threat to Soviet hegemony. Ironically, Gheorghiu-Dej benefited from his own party's lack of popular support. Had Romanian interwar communism been a vibrant force, Stalin would have almost certainly purged the home communists and Gheorghiu-Dej.

Secondly, the 1952 purges were a likely outcome when one considers the nature of the 1944 coup. Unlike other Eastern European countries after the war, Romania's internal political structures were not immediately destroyed. The Soviet Union needed the home communists, and from the very beginning, they possessed power that was usually only reserved for Muscovite communists. The Soviets developed ties with the home communists, and as the years passed, these ties with them became stronger while the ties with the Muscovite communists became weaker and so the Pauker group was expendable. The Soviets no longer needed political alternatives as was the case in the mid-1940s. Gheorghiu-Dej had proven himself a devout Stalinist, and he had enough support to push through Soviet economic and industrial plans but not enough to pose a serious threat. Pauker's lack of popularity was seen as a contributing factor to the failure of the collectivization program.

NATIONALISM AND THE NEW COURSE: 1953–1956

Following the 1952 purges, the PMR started advocating its own brand of Romanian communism. The death of Stalin marked the conclusion of an era in which Gheorghiu-Dej's power in the PMR increased and consolidated. In an attempt to increase its popularity with the people and decrease its dependence on the Soviets, the party stressed the primacy of Romanian needs. The so-called New Course provided the PMR with a less restrictive atmosphere to press its claims. Romanian nationalism became inevitably linked to economics, and it was during this period that the country's opposition to the economic policies of the Council for Mutual Economic Assistance (Comecon) and the influence of China became significant issues. Gheorghiu-Dej was able to exploit the growing tension between the Soviet Union and China. The brief period of the New Course occurred between the death of Stalin and the Soviet 20th Party Congress. The Soviets de-emphasized strict compliance to their model in favor of more individualistic models. This is not to say that the Eastern European countries developed independently of the Soviet Union; rather, they developed individually within Soviet parameters.

The New Course was a consequence of the struggles in the Kremlin. Khrushchev and Malenkov were competing for party power, and Eastern Europe was an important political issue. Khrushchev attempted to replace Eastern European leaderships that were dominated by Stalin's supporters. He hoped that by purging the Stalinists (Muscovite communists), he could establish his own support. He was building the same kind of support in Eastern Europe that Stalin possessed but based on different principles.

Ideologically, Gheorghiu-Dej was not a home communist. He subscribed to a Stalinist economic and political model. Even though the Romanian regime was lead by home communists, Khrushchev did not support it. He wanted to destroy the power of these "little Stalins," but in the case of Romania, Gheorghiu-Dej manipulated the New Course and consolidated his power. He was one of the first Eastern European leaders to adopt the New Course, but this created a need to critically assess the party's industrialization policy.[13] The leadership was confronted with the problem of finding someone to blame for the party's failed economic and political policies. The previous answer had always been the Pauker group; however, the party hesitated in placing all the blame on the Muscovites. While Gheorghiu-Dej stated during the purges that the Pauker group had manipulated the party organs, now that he had consolidated his power he was more reluctant to directly address party mistakes. He viewed the question of party manipulation as a "Pandora's box" best kept closed.

Therefore, Gheorghiu-Dej had to find another scapegoat for the failures of the past. He blamed the government and not the party for the economic failures. At the Central Committee plenum in August 1953, a resolution was issued which denounced the rate of industrialization.[14] The resolution stated that heavy industrialization had proceeded too quickly. The underlying problem with industrialization was identified as the rate of investment, which had far exceeded what the economy could support. In addition, economic resources were not wisely allocated. Inefficient factories had amassed huge deficits while the agricultural and consumer segments of the economy received limited funding. This dichotomy caused the standard of living among workers to stagnate. Those few consumer goods that could be found were often far too expensive for the average worker (this situation was repeated in the 1980s). The major problem facing the economy in 1953 was the imposition of an investment scale that was not suited to the economy.

Part of the problem was that an enormous part of the national income was being sent directly to the Soviet Union. The Sovroms and reparation payments were depleting the economy. However, economic mismanagement was considered the primary cause of poor economic performance. The blame for this mismanagement was attributed to the Ministry of Finance, and by implication, Luca. Although Gheorghiu-Dej did not expressly mention Luca, his attacks on the Ministry of Finance left little doubt who he felt was responsible for the economy's failure. He argued that the party could not be held responsible for the economic mismanagement. In this way, he used the government and indirectly the Muscovite communists as the scapegoats for the economic failures and in doing so sought to emphasize that this economic failure was not the fault of the party's leading organs (e.g., the Central Committee and the Politburo).

Gheorghiu-Dej also criticized the party's regional and front organizations. The Bucharest regional organization was especially criticized for its lack of collective leadership. The first secretary of the City Committee Bureau was accused of centralizing decision-making into his own hands.[15] What makes this attack so interesting is that Pauker had been in control of the Bucharest organization. Gheorghiu-Dej was again indirectly implicating the Muscovites. Party front organizations were criticized for not forming links between the party and the people. Trade unions were attacked for not being the "transmission belts" of society. The front organizations were easy targets because they had neglected the concerns of the peasants and were considered responsible for the alienation of the peasants from the party. Although the leadership indirectly criticized the party, the criticisms were limited to the regional level and the front organizations. The organizations that were the real decision-making bodies within the PMR were not directly criticized.

With these attacks, Gheorghiu-Dej manipulated the state and party hierarchy. After the death of Stalin, the idea of collective leadership was accepted throughout Eastern Europe. State and party power were separated, and therefore Gheorghiu-Dej relinquished his post as first secretary in 1954, but he had his close associate, Apostol, appointed to the position. Gheorghiu-Dej still retained his position as premier. Interestingly, almost all other Eastern European leaders retained their party position.[16] Later in 1955, he took back the party post and appointed Stoica premier. This game of political musical chairs underscores how powerful he was by the mid-1950s.

NATIONALISM AND SOVIET POLITICS

In Eastern Europe, nationalism grew during the period of the New Course, and Romania was no exception. Nationalism had always played a role in the country's politics. The party promoted national concerns for two reasons. Firstly, nationalism was a "quick fix" for the party's deeply rooted problem of popular support. The party preyed upon the natural prejudices and fears of the people. The 1952 purges linked the home communists with traditional Romanian values. Party leaders identified themselves as national communists and the Muscovites as foreigners. Aside from appealing to prejudice, the party later enacted economic measures to bolster its popularity. The second reason why the PMR promoted nationalism was to decrease its reliance on the Soviet Union for support. As the links between the party and the people were strengthened, the need for Soviet support diminished. The party attempted to build its legitimacy based on Romanian populism not Soviet authority.

The character of Romanian nationalism has been extensively debated. There have been various interpretations regarding the nature of Romanian nationalist attacks on the Soviet Union. Stephen Fischer-Galati argues that the "postwar mass opposition to Communism cannot be characterized as an overtly anti-Russian phenomenon. It was anti-Russian only by identification of Russia with Communism."[17] Although Gheorghiu-Dej was not in a position to attack the Soviet leadership directly he was, by the mid-1950s, in a position to resist Soviet demands for more conformity. However to oppose Soviet demands, the PMR needed to further develop popular support. The accession of Khrushchev posed a threat to Gheorghiu-Dej's leadership.

Under Gheorghiu-Dej, nationalism took on a historical element. He linked the 1952 purges with the 1944 coup. He made the coup the starting point of Romanian communist nationalism. He blurred the realities of the coup to increase not only the role of the home communists but also the party's popular support. His interpretation also diminished the role of the Soviet army. In August 1955, Khrushchev visited Romania for the eleventh anniversary of the coup. The occasion was marked by a disagreement between him and Gheorghiu-Dej. Khrushchev insisted that there should be a division of functions between the party and the state.[18]

Gheorghiu-Dej's response to this attack was rather strident. He stated that the Chinese supported the party's interpretation of the 1944 coup. Furthermore, he argued that they supported the Romanian view on the individual roads of socialism. This was the first time the Chinese became a factor in Romanian politics, but by the 1960s the Chinese would become an important foreign policy player. This episode demonstrated that Gheorghiu-Dej felt secure in his party position. This security was partly based on the failure of Khrushchev to supplant him. Khrushchev could not implement pre-emptive de-Stalinization in Romania, and his inability to remove or even censure the leadership increased Gheorghiu-Dej's influence in the party and among the people. Almost every other Eastern European country went through, in varying degrees, some de-Stalinization. In Romania, no meaningful de-Stalinization occurred. There were three reasons why de-Stalinization did not occur.

Firstly, there were no ardent anti-Stalinists in the leadership. Whereas there were Stalinist and anti-Stalinist factions in almost every other Eastern European country, Gheorghiu-Dej benefited from the party cohesion. While there were challenges to his leadership, these challenges emanated from nationalist not anti-Stalinist forces. The most likely candidate to lead Khrushchev's campaign of de-Stalinization would have been Patrascanu, but he was executed in 1954. The only other possible anti-Stalinist candidate would have been Pauker, but she had been removed in the 1952 purges. Khrushchev simply did not have a candidate to seriously challenge Gheorghiu-Dej.

Secondly, the party feared the consequences of de-Stalinization. Because the party's support among the population was so tenuous, even those in the lower echelons, who might have favored a change in the leadership, were concerned that de-Stalinization would open the flood gates and that they too would be swept away by the current of de-Stalinization. Party members feared that the population would interpret de-Stalinization as de-communization.

Thirdly, de-Stalinization propaganda was not successful with the people because of the PMR's policies. Romanian leaders anticipated a challenge from Moscow and used economic incentives to increase their support among the people.[19] On the other hand, they also used the secret police to maintain control. Khrushchev was unable to use the people as an instrument of de-Stalinization.

Although Gheorghiu-Dej rejected the substance of Khrushchev's New Course policies, he had to in principle support the program. For example at the Second Party Congress in December of 1955, he stated that the party completely supported the idea of peaceful coexistence.[20] He argued that it was in the interests of the party to maintain close ties with other Eastern bloc countries in order to attain the country's national goals.

ECONOMICS AND THE NEW COURSE

The New Course marked the beginning of an economic division within Eastern Europe. The first apparent economic dispute between Romania and other Eastern European countries occurred shortly after the death of Stalin. The dispute was based on the New Course policy of increasing the agricultural products available in the domestic economy to prevent any popular unrest that might result from the relaxation of Stalinist terror. In Romania, agricultural exports were reduced to increase the domestic availability of foodstuffs and other primary commodities.[21]

The PMR believed that an increase in basic consumer goods would pacify the population; however, other Eastern European countries also needed these items. This situation greatly increased the antagonism between these countries and Romania. The reduction in foodstuff exports, however, had another consequence. Without the capital generated from these exports, Romanian imports of Eastern bloc machinery equipment decreased dramatically. Between 1953 and 1956, imports of Czechoslovak machinery declined by almost 80%.[22]

Romania's reduction in trade had a ripple effect throughout the Eastern European economies. The country was severely criticized by these countries and the Soviet Union for its economic policies; however, these policies were dictated in large part by the Soviet exploitation of the Romanian economy. As a part of the New Course, most Eastern European countries saw their war reparations discontinued and the dissolution of joint-stock companies. Romania and Hungary had the most joint-stock companies, and Romania was one of the last Eastern European countries to have its companies dissolved. This is one of the reasons why the economy did not grow at the same rate as other Eastern European countries.

Industrialization became important because it offered the Romanian leadership the possibility of greater economic independence. Industrial policy was oriented towards providing the economy, as well as the leadership, with autonomy in the Eastern bloc and by implication autonomy from the Soviet Union. Emphasis was placed on industrial development, and the capital that would have been used in purchasing imports was to be invested in industry. Trade policy was based on a policy of economic reciprocity with other Eastern European countries. The Ministry of Foreign Trade had a strong preference for buying machines and equipment from countries that would in return purchase Romanian industrial products.[23] However, not all countries engaged in this form of trade. Czechoslovakia, for example, argued that Romania manufactured the same industrial equipment that its own industries produced (and of an inferior quality) and would not purchase the country's industrial goods. Other countries, such as the Soviet Union and East Germany participated, and this program of reciprocity allowed Romania to build its industries at a substantially faster rate. In addition, the policy also decreased the party's economic dependence on the Soviet Union. However, countries such as Czechoslovakia wanted greater economic integration based on comparative advantage, and Comecon became the focus of economic policy disputes in the 1950s and 1960s.

COMECON

Stalin established Comecon in 1949 as a response to the Marshall Plan. He did not want Eastern Europe to receive Western aid and created Comecon in order for the Soviet Union to rebuild Eastern European postwar economies. However up until 1955, it was relegated to creating bilateral agreements between Eastern European member-states. It was not until late 1955 and early 1956 that Comecon started working on a pattern of multilateral economic specialization. This plan was developed to create a balance between Eastern European supply and demand.

By the mid-1950s, Romanian economic policies were harming the Czechoslovakian economy. In February of 1956, Czechoslovakia issued a directive, supposedly to assist the industrialization efforts of the lesser-developed countries (LDCs), calling for a study of the division of labor among the Eastern bloc countries.[24] During this time, many articles were published that criticized the economic policies of LDCs, and although these articles never referred to a specific country, there was little doubt that much of the criticism was aimed at Romania.

During the New Course there were three distinct groups emerging within Comecon: the most developed countries (East Germany and Czechoslovakia), the more developed countries (Hungary and Poland) and the LDCs (Bulgaria and Romania). In the 1950s, the major issue facing Comecon concerned economies of scale. A dispute emerged in the Eastern bloc over the production of low-technology items (e.g., tractors, trucks and lathes). These items, when produced in large quantities, provided significant economies of scale and were highly profitable. The LDCs wanted to increase their production of these goods. Of course the more developed countries wanted to protect their dominance in these industries. This debate became more intense following events in 1956.

ROMANIAN DE-STALINIZATION

Khrushchev's 1956 secret speech given at the Soviet 20th Party Congress was a turning point in international communism. The speech denounced Stalin and his practices, especially his cult of personality. In March 1956 the Central Committee of the PMR held an enlarged plenum to discuss the speech. Gheorghiu-Dej made general criticisms of Stalin's cult of personality and accused the Pauker group of being Stalinists. He argued that they had created a personality cult in the PMR. Furthermore, he stated that they had manipulated and abused the party organs. Gheorghiu-Dej argued, using his particular theory of Stalinism, that the Pauker group had been purged before 1956, and therefore the PMR was one of the first Eastern European parties to undergo de-Stalinization.

By making this argument, he blocked any attempt by Moscow to purge the party. During a time when the Soviets were purging other Eastern European parties, the PMR leadership remained intact. This further increased the party's cohesion; however, Gheorghiu-Dej still received challenges to his leadership and his interpretation of de-Stalinization. Some Central Committee members attacked him for Stalinist policies. They attacked his economic policies and misuse of power. However, he used the fear of removal from the Central Committee or even the party to silence his critics.

The Soviet Union was not supportive of Gheorghiu-Dej's interpretation of de-Stalinization, but he was allowed to pay mere lip service to de-Stalinization because of events in other Eastern European countries.

During 1956 there were uprisings in both Poland and Hungary, and these events posed a threat to Soviet hegemony in Eastern Europe and a serious threat to Khrushchev's leadership. Many in the Kremlin attributed these uprisings to Khrushchev's de-Stalinization program and New Course politics. After the uprisings, the Soviet emphasis changed from de-Stalinization to stability in Eastern Europe. The Soviets felt that at least the Romanian regime was stable, and Gheorghiu-Dej's Stalinist tendencies were tolerated. Gheorghiu-Dej used the uprisings in Poland and Hungary as the pretext for a party purge. He argued that certain individuals in the party leadership were unreliable and could incite dissention within the party and the country.

THE 1957 PURGES

The 1957 purges solidified Gheorghiu-Dej's leadership of the party and were aimed at his two most influential party opponents: Iosif Chisinevschi and Miron Constantinescu. Chisinevschi was chief of propaganda, and Constantinescu was organizational secretary and minister of culture. Both had opposed his interpretation of de-Stalinization and wanted to implement the message of the 20th Party Congress.[25] Purging these men allowed Gheorghiu-Dej to eliminate the last dangerous element of the left (Chisinevschi) and the most popular advocate of reform (Constantinescu). Chisinevschi and Constantinescu knew that they were not in a position to actually oust Gheorghiu-Dej; rather, they wanted to generate support in the Central Committee for the adoption of more liberal policies.[26] This would have increased their prestige and influence in the party, and they would have been able to press their claims for elevation in the party hierarchy.

Gheorghiu-Dej realized that the Romanian people and the Soviets did not regard these men as Stalinists. So at the June 1957 Central Committee plenum, he argued that Constantinescu's liberal position was only a guise to mask his Stalinist tendencies. To make the charges seem as if they were coming from the party and not just one man, he had other party members attack Chisinevschi and Constantinescu as devout Stalinists. At that time, the party hierarchy was composed of factions with only subtle policy differences. However, the Chisinevschi-Constantinescu faction represented a major break with party politics. Party authority was based on the maintenance of cohesion, and the leadership feared that the proposed reforms would destroy the party's cohesion. Both men were purged from the party, and while the 1957 purges did not totally eliminate challenges to

Gheorghiu-Dej's leadership, they did eliminate the last important faction opposed to his policies.

TRADE POLICY

In 1959, Premier Ion Maurer made a tour of Western Europe exploring possible trade and credit relations. Within a year, negotiations between Romania and Britain were conducted on long-standing compensation claims. In the next three years (1958–1961), Western foreign trade increased approximately 70%.[27] From 1958 until 1961, trade with Britain, Belgium, Sweden and Switzerland more than tripled. Trade with West Germany increased a staggering 133%, surpassing trade with East Germany.[28] During this same period trade with the Soviet Union increased only 12%.

East Germany and Czechoslovakia repeatedly chastised "certain socialist countries" for ideologically incorrect trading practices. The more industrialized Eastern European countries were furious about Romania's trading practices with Western Europe and the United States because the country was trading its timber and foodstuff products with the West for machinery equipment. These trade practices provided the PMR with two benefits. Firstly, the expansion of industrial trade increased Romania's capital base (due to the economies of scale). This increase in capital enabled the country to reduce its trade deficit. Romania also reinvested the capital back into the industrialization program, which allowed the country to industrialize at an even faster pace. Secondly while the country was still heavily dependent on the Soviet Union, the new trade agreements made it less dependent on Comecon members for industrial products. Romania was increasing its Western trade while other Eastern European countries were decreasing their Western trade.

VIEW OF THE WARSAW TREATY ORGANIZATION

The party's policy towards the Warsaw Treaty Organization (Warsaw Pact) was a logical extension of its rejection of supranational planning in Comecon. Romania's differences with the Warsaw Pact can be traced as far back as 1955.[29] Gheorghiu-Dej wanted Soviet troops removed from the country because their presence symbolically illustrated the party's reliance on Moscow for its authority. In October 1956, the Soviets announced that they would examine their troop deployment policy in Warsaw Pact member-states. The Romanians and the Soviets negotiated over troop withdrawal until December with little success. During the negotiations, the Soviets made general comments about Eastern bloc sovereignty and equality, but the PMR did not achieve the removal of Soviet troops.

The Romanians, however, continued to press for withdrawal. Finally in May 1958, the Warsaw Pact Political Consultative Committee decided to remove the troops.[30] The decision seems partially based on the growing importance of China in international communism. In March 1958, a Romanian delegation journeyed to China. The Romanians were well aware of the increasing tensions between the Chinese and the Soviets, and one of the major topics of discussion between the Romanians and the Chinese was the removal of Soviet troops from socialist countries. They concluded their discussions with the following joint statement: "The military blocs in Europe and Asia should be abolished and replaced by systems of collective security; military bases established on foreign territory should be eliminated; and armed forces stationed on foreign territory should be withdrawn."[31] The Romanians cleverly used this statement to support their demand for the troop withdrawal.

Although the schism in Sino-Soviet relations was a factor in the Soviet decision to remove troops from the country, it was not the only one. In addition, the Soviets felt secure in removing troops because of Romania's geographical position relative to the Soviet Union. The country had only one open border, with Yugoslavia. The rest of Romania's borders were with Warsaw Pact countries. In addition, the Soviet Union had troops stationed just over the boarder in the Soviet Republic of Moldavia. Therefore, the Soviets still maintained an important *external* military threat.

POLICIES IN THE 1960s: THE RETURN OF NATIONALISM

In March 1960, Gheorghiu-Dej merged the leadership positions of the party and the government. The merging of these posts was in direct conflict with the Soviet desire for collective leadership. At the Romanian Third Party Congress in June 1960, Gheorghiu-Dej urged the acceptance of a proposed six-year plan. This plan called for the further development of heavy industry. The PMR concluded that the only way to block Soviet attempts at economic specialization was to engage in rapid industrialization.[32] By the end of 1960, industrial production was 67% above the 1955 level.[33] The Third Party Congress was a watershed in the country's industrial program. Gheorghiu-Dej argued that the strength of the socialist camp was directly proportional to the strength of the individual members. Furthermore, he maintained that each country was better qualified to determine its own economic policies. The Third Party Congress marked a return of nationalism that had a decidedly anti-Soviet element.

There are three reasons why the PMR identified itself with nationalism. Firstly, the nationalist policies increased the party's popular support. Secondly, the policies were directly associated with Romania's political struggle with the Soviet Union over economic policies in Comecon and general autonomy in foreign affairs. Thirdly, the leadership believed that these policies would create greater economic success. As a corollary to these policies, the PMR also increased the party's membership. During the most important stage of the Comecon dispute (April 1962 through December 1964), party membership increased dramatically (see Table 2.1).[34]

Unlike the nationalism associated with the New Course, Romanian nationalism in the 1960s was more anti-Soviet, but the party had to avoid provoking a military response by the Soviet Union. In the early 1960s, the government instituted several measures that were clearly anti-Soviet: Russian language requirements were dropped from school curricula, and the names of streets, institutions and theaters were changed from Russian to Romanian. There are a number of reasons why the Soviets allowed the expression of Romanian nationalism. Firstly, the Soviets did not have troops actually stationed in the country. While it would have been easy for the Soviets to launch an attack from across the border, the political ramifications might have been severe. After the Hungarian uprising in 1956, an invasion of Romania might have had international consequences that the Soviet Union would have wanted to avoid. Secondly, the Soviets were much more concerned with the Sino-Soviet dispute than with Romania. This dispute threatened the Soviet Union's primacy in the international communist movement, and the Romanians were very adept at using this dispute for their own political gain.

Thirdly, Romanian trade policies made the country less dependent on the Soviet Union. The country developed trade relations with the West that decreased its dependency on Comecon trading partners. This meant that the Soviet Union could exert less economic pressure. For example, Romania had become virtually self-sufficient in the production of energy. Finally, the cohesion in the PMR provided the party with a core of support against Soviet demands. The 1952 and 1957 purges had left Gheorghiu-Dej in control of a unified party.

COMECON AND FOREIGN TRADE

During the 1950s, the Soviets had allowed the Romanians a great deal of latitude in their economic policies. Comecon integration was not forced, but in the early 1960s the Soviets pressed their demands for economic specialization. Soviet domestic growth slowed down in the early 1960s, and the Soviets believed that economic specialization would provide a boost to their sluggish economy. In addition, their trade requirements shifted. Comecon integration and the socialist division of labor were predicated not only on Khrushchev's desire for more political unity within Eastern Europe, but also on the Soviet need to eliminate Stalinist economic policies. Khrushchev believed that comparative advantage should dictate Eastern European industrial policy.

The Romanians were quite aware of the political ramifications of Comecon policy and sought to weaken the internal structure of Comecon. The 1960 Comecon statutes illustrate the inherent deficiency of the organization. The statutes stressed the principle of voluntary cooperation and participation of member-states. Any member-state could refuse to implement a proposal, and because of the voluntary nature of Comecon the Romanians could unilaterally reject economic specialization.

In 1962 the Soviets increased their pressure on the Romanian leadership. In June, a Comecon meeting was held to discuss Khrushchev's plan for greater economic planning. The Soviets, as well as the East Germans and Czechs, pressed for greater economic authority for Comecon. Khrushchev wanted economic planning based on multilateral agreements. In other words, he wanted Comecon to conduct supranational planning and to enforce its decisions on member-states.

This meeting produced a joint declaration entitled "The Basic Principles of the Internal Division of Labor." The document was signed by all Comecon members, including Romania. The declaration stressed economic cooperation between members and stated that Comecon would become a supranational institution. Comecon would coordinate the economies of the various members. The Romanians were able, however, to get a concession from the Soviets. In exchange for signing the declaration, they pressed for a statement of principles, and at a June 1962 meeting the organization established the Comecon Principles. They reiterated the same practices that were stated in the 1960 Comecon statutes and included voluntary cooperation and a unanimous voting requirement. These principles effectively reduced the power and influence of the previous declaration. Economic coordination would still be based on the voluntary cooperation of each member, and thus Romania successfully blocked the Soviet attempt at economic integration. These 1962 meetings did not produce any reconciliation between the Comecon members, and in fact the acrimony between members increased.

The Soviets placed a great deal of emphasis on Romanian integration into Comecon because Romania was the only country that opposed economic specialization. Poland and Hungary would certainly have received only mixed benefits from further integration. Polish leader Gomulka knew that his country was, in many ways, in the same economic position as Romania, but his devotion to the Soviet leadership prevented him from articulating his doubts. Hungary clearly was not in a position to voice concerns after 1956. Moreover, the Hungarians did not want a strong and prosperous Romania. Hungary felt that a growing Romanian economy would pacify the ethnic Hungarian minority in Transylvania. Bulgaria had the most to lose from economic integration. Being the least developed Comecon member, Bulgaria desperately needed to modernize its industrial sector. Economic specialization would not have allowed Bulgaria to develop its industries and capital base, but the country was extremely loyal to the Soviet Union and supported Comecon.

Gheorghiu-Dej knew that Khrushchev was determined to integrate Romania into Comecon. In August 1962, Khrushchev authored an article in a Soviet magazine explaining the need for greater cooperation among Comecon members. While the article made general comments about economic integration, there was no doubt that much of the article was directed at Romania. Khrushchev argued that integration was vital for socialist development, and he concluded that the "measures for deepening the international division of labor, for greater cooperation and specialization of products will increase the interrelationship and interdependence of the national economies of the countries belonging to [Comecon]."[35] Economic interdependence was exactly what the PMR feared. The autonomy of the Romanian leadership would be jeopardized by integration into Comecon.

The February 1963 Comecon meeting was a watershed in Romanian-Soviet relations. In February the vice premiers of the member-states met in Moscow to discuss economic specialization and supranational planning. During this meeting, a disagreement occurred between the Romanian delegation and the other delegations. The division was so serious that the PMR called a meeting of the Central Committee after their delegation returned. The Central Committee, for the first time, publicly acknowledged the division between Comecon members and affirmed the position that the Romanian delegation had taken in Moscow. The delegation stressed bilateralism rather than multilateralism and economic sovereignty rather than economic interdependence.

At a May 1963 Comecon meeting, the Soviets attempted to produce an agreement with the Romanian delegation. Khrushchev's inability to exert control was undermining his position and influence in Comecon and Moscow. The Romanians would not agree to any proposal that the Soviets or other Comecon members introduced. Later, Khrushchev sent a Soviet delegation to Bucharest to negotiate a Comecon policy. Ceausescu was the Romanian representative to the meeting, and he reiterated the Romanian position on industrialization and economic planning.[36]

The Soviet leadership was faced with a dilemma. Without raw materials and foodstuffs from Romania, Comecon integration and supranational planning would be impossible. On the other hand, the Soviets had been unsuccessful in pressing their demands for economic integration. Finally in July 1963, they decided to end their demand for supranational planning. The July meeting of Comecon members ended with a statement declaring that the coordination of the member-state economies would be delayed. It also affirmed the prior commitment to bilateral agreements and the principle of equality among its members. The statement spoke of the sovereignty of each nation in its economic planning and was a major retrenchment in Soviet policy. Khrushchev could not force Romania to agree to his demands, and this was seen as a victory for Gheorghiu-Dej and a defeat for Khrushchev. After Khrushchev's removal, the new Soviet leadership signed agreements with Romania providing technical assistance and finally supporting the country's industrialization program. Therefore by the end of 1964, Gheorghiu-Dej had successfully pressed his claims for industrialization and economic autonomy. The Comecon dispute had increased the stature of his leadership both at home and in the West.

THE 1964 STATEMENT

The "Statement on the Stand of the Romanian Workers' Party Concerning the Problems of the World Communist and Working-Class Movement" was published by the PMR Central Committee in April of 1964. This document became known as the "Romanian declaration of independence." It explained the country's position in world communism. The document criticized the Comintern policies of the 1920s and the 1930s, and noted how the Comintern had prevented the party from forming links with the people. The PMR argued that communist states should work closely together but not under interstate authority. Furthermore, the document stated that no country should present its interests as the interests of the entire socialist bloc. The Central Committee contended that there were commonalties that linked communist countries; however, no country should impose its pattern of development on another country. Ostensibly the leadership was addressing the issue of the Comintern, but there was little doubt that the declaration was directed at the recent Comecon dispute. This document was important because it asserted the right of each communist country to decide its own policies. It argued that for each country, the needs of the citizens and of the country came before all other allegiances. The Romanians were arguing for a more developed form of nationalism.

CONCLUSION

Gheorghiu-Dej successfully transformed one of the weakest Eastern European communist parties into a much more cohesive and autonomous organization. Although he died in March of 1965, he lived long enough to see his vision of autonomy implemented. Romanian political development did not follow the Eastern European pattern. The first indication of the country's uniqueness occurred during the mid-1940s, and culminated in the 1952 purges of the Pauker group, an event that is extremely important in the development of the country's autonomy. If Pauker and Luca had continued in leadership positions, they might have eventually supplanted Gheorghiu-Dej, and Romania would have embarked on a totally different political course. Issues such as de-Stalinization, Comecon policy and the Sino-Soviet dispute were matters that involved every Eastern European country. Gheorghiu-Dej was able to blend nationalism and Soviet ideology turning issues that challenged his authority to political advantage. Romanian autonomy was the legacy that Gheorghiu-Dej left to his "apprentice" and eventual successor, Ceausescu.[37]

1   Keith Hitchens, *Romania 1866–1947* (Oxford: Clarendon Press, 1994), p. 495.
2   The political importance of the August 1944 coup was not lost on Ceausescu. After the death of Gheorghiu-Dej in 1965 the party under the direction of Ceausescu, revised the historical

account of the coup. This revision noted the important role of noncommunist parties and reduced the importance of the PCR in the arrest of Antonescu. Ceausescu revised the role of the party to reduce the influence of the Gheorghiu-Dej and more importantly his living supporters.

3   Tismaneanu argues that the Pauker group's influence waned in late 1944. See, Vladimir Tismaneanu, "The Road to Cominform: Internationalism, Factionalism, and National Communism in Romania, 1944–1948," *Sfera politicii*, December 1992, p. 15.

4   Stelian Neagoe, *Istoria Guvernelor Romaniei* (Bucharest: Editura Machiavelli, 1995), pp. 153–154.

5   For a discussion of the Radescu government see, Dinu C. Giurescu, *Guvernarea Nicolae Radescu* (Bucharest: Editura All, 1996). For a general discussion concerning the events of 1946 and 1947 see, Monica Lovinescu, Virgil Ierunc and Serban Papacostea, "Anul electoral 1946," 22, 1–21 May 1996, pp. 12–14.

6   *Romania retragerea trupelor Sovietice 1958* (Bucharest: Editura Didactica si Pedagogica, 1996), p. 58.

7   Ghita Ionescu, *Communism in Rumania: 1944–1962* (Oxford: Oxford University Press, 1964), p. 200.

8   Robert R. King, *History of the Romanian Communist Party* (Stanford, CA: Hoover Institution Press, 1980), p. 73.

9   Ghita Ionescu, *Communism in Rumania: 1944–1962*, p. 209.

10   Ibid, p. 210.

11   Michael Shafir, *Romania: Politics, Economics and Society* (Boulder, CO: Lynne Reinner Publishers, 1985), p. 66.

12   However, the party organs were not monolithic. Mary Ellen Fischer argues that the composition of the Central Committee during this time was far from homogeneous. See, Mary Ellen Fischer, "The Romanian Communist Party and Its Central Committee: Patterns of Growth and Change," *Southeastern Europe*, June 1979, pp. 1–28.

13   Stephen Fischer-Galati, *Twentieth Century Rumania*, 2nd ed. (New York: Columbia University Press, 1991), p. 131.

14   Ghita Ionescu, *Communism in Rumania: 1944–1962*, p. 223.

15   Ibid, p. 227.

16   Andrew Gyorgy, "The Internal Political Order," in Stephen Fischer-Galati, ed., *Eastern Europe in the Sixties* (New York: Praeger, 1963), p. 77.

17   Stephen Fischer-Galati, "Rumania: A Dissenting Voice in the Balkans," in Andrew Gyorgy, ed., *Issues of World Communism* (Princeton, NJ: Van Nostrand Co., 1966), p. 129.

18   Stephen Fischer-Galati, *Twentieth Century Rumania*, 2nd ed., p. 141.

19   Trond Gilberg, "The Communist Party of Romania," in Stephen Fischer-Galati, ed., *The Communist Parties of Eastern Europe* (New York: Columbia University Press, 1979), p. 283.

20   Stephen Fischer-Galati, "Rumania: A Dissenting Voice in the Balkans," p. 132.

21   John Michael Montias, "Background and Origins of the Rumanian Dispute with Comecon," *Soviet Studies*, October 1964, p. 127.

22   John Michael Montias, *Economic Development in Communist Rumania* (Cambridge, MA: M.I.T. Press, 1967), p. 189.

23   John Michael Montias, "Background and Origins of the Rumanian Dispute with Comecon," p. 128.

24   John Michael Montias, *Economic Development in Communist Rumania*, p. 190.

25   Paul Lendvai, *Eagles in the Cobwebs: Nationalism and Communism in the Balkans* (Garden City, NY: Doubleday, 1969), p. 291.

26   J. F. Brown, *The New Eastern Europe: The Khrushchev Era and After* (New York: Praeger, 1966), p. 67.

27   John Michael Montias, "Background and Origins of the Rumanian Dispute with Comecon," p. 136.

28   Ibid.

29   Robin Remington, *The Warsaw Pact: Case Studies in Communist Conflict Resolution* (Cambridge, MA: M.I.T. Press, 1971), p. 57.

30 *Romania retragerea trupelor Sovietice 1958*, pp. 280–281.

31 Robin Remington, *The Warsaw Pact: Case Studies in Communist Conflict Resolution*, p. 62.

32 Stephen Fischer-Galati, "Rumania and the Sino-Soviet Conflict," in Kurt London, ed., *Eastern Europe in Transition* (Baltimore, MD: The Johns Hopkins University Press, 1966), p. 269.

33 David Floyd, *Rumania: Russia's Dissident Ally* (New York: Praeger, 1965), p. 59.

34 John Michael Montias, *Economic Development in Communist Rumania*, p. 204.

35 N. S. Khrushchev, "Vital Questions of the Development of the World Socialist System," *The Current Digest of the Soviet Press*, 3 October 1962, p. 3

36 John Michael Montias, *Economic Development in Communist Rumania*, p. 215.

37 Mary Ellen Fischer, *Nicolae Ceausescu: A Study in Political Leadership* (Boulder, CO: Lynne Rienner, 1989), p. 5.

Chapter 3

HISTORY OF ROMANIA: 1965–1989

The rhetoric and symbols of Romanian communism used by Gheorghiu-Dej in the late 1950s and throughout the 1960s grew to an absurd level during the Ceausescu regime. From the early 1970s until his death in 1989, Ceausescu established the most pervasive Eastern European cult of personality. He manipulated Romanian politics, economic policy and even the West in his quest for absolute power. He utilized the Romanian secret police, the *securitate*, to suppress all opposition to his leadership and used them also to enlist the population to inform on each other. Ceausescu manipulated his close relationship with Western leaders to provide Romania with greater foreign policy autonomy, but by the mid-1980s the West had become his harshest critic. Ceausescu's reaction to the changes in Eastern Europe in November and December 1989 demonstrated how isolated he had become. While the circumstances surrounding the Romanian revolution in December 1989 are still unclear, there is no doubt that by the time of his death, Ceausescu had alienated domestic groups that were essential to his very survival.

The irony is that Ceausescu in the late 1960s and the early 1970s was considered one of the most enlightened Eastern European leaders. During this period, he reformed the domestic economy (the production of consumer products was a priority), and his foreign policy was widely hailed in the West. Two American presidents and countless Western European heads of state visited Romania. Ceausescu also developed a reputation as an internantional negotiator, particularly in the Middle East. This chapter examines Ceausescu's cult of personality and its impact on society, the economy and ethnic minorities.

SUCCESSION AND COLLECTIVE LEADERSHIP

After the death of Gheorghiu-Dej in March 1965, the PMR confronted the issue of succession. Similar to the situation in the Soviet Union in 1953, Gheorghiu-Dej had not designated anyone in the leadership as his heir.[1] No individual had enough support to assume his position in the party and the state, and the PMR wanted to ensure a smooth transition of power. The party's primary concern was to maintain its authority and prevent opposition groups from forming.

Therefore, the succession struggle was a private struggle conducted within the party.

By March 1965, there were several individuals in the Gheorghiu-Dej inner circle that were likely candidates to replace the party leader, including Ceausescu, Stoica, Apostol, Maurer and Alexandru Draghici. In March 1965, the PMR Politburo, the party's highest organ, recommended to the Central Committee that Ceausescu be named first secretary, and he was quickly appointed. The Central Committee recommended to the Grand National Assembly that Stoica be selected as president of the Council of State (unofficially, president of the country). Maurer maintained his position of president of the Council of Ministers (prime minister).[2] Whereas Gheorghiu-Dej had jointly held the position of first secretary and president of the Council of State, this period of succession involved collective leadership.

As first secretary, Ceausescu initiated changes to the party's statutes to increase the power of party officials over state institutions and as a consequence increase his power over rivals.[3] However, the emphasis in the party between 1965 and 1967 was on collective leadership. For example at the Ninth Party Congress in July 1965, a change enacted in the party statutes prohibited an individual from holding positions in the state and the party organs. The position of first secretary was renamed general secretary indicating that no individual was "first" within the party. To indicate a break with the previous regime, the Congress renamed the party the Romanian Communist Party (*Partidul Comunist Roman* or PCR). The name was enshrined in the new constitution approved in August 1965.[4]

The Congress also adopted the creation of a new Political Executive Committee (a larger version of the Politburo) and a smaller Presidium (a decision-making body selected from the Political Executive Committee). Ceausescu argued that these two new party organs would facilitate collective leadership and prevent the possibility of any one individual amassing to much power. However in his position as general secretary Ceausescu eventually made use of these party organs, replacing those loyal to Gheorghiu-Dej with his own supporters.

Aside from the adoption of a collective leadership, the other significant decision taken at the Congress was to launch a formal investigation into those arrested during the Gheorghiu-Dej regime. Michael Shafir argues that as part of the "Beria syndrome," Gheorghiu-Dej's successors were concerned about the influence of Draghici, the minister of internal affairs.[5] Because he was head of the

Romanian secret police, he was considered by all possible successors as the biggest threat. As a result of the changes in the party statutes, Draghici was forced to relinquish his position in the ministry and join the Secretariat.

The other serious rival to Ceausescu was Apostol, who had served as first deputy prime minister since 1961. He had been regarded by many within the party as Gheorghiu-Dej's most likely successor.[6] In fact during the Ninth Party Congress, Apostol was the only individual that voiced a different opinion from the collective leadership and Ceausescu over the creation of new party organs.[7] But because Ceausescu had invoked the idea of collective leadership to justify the creation of these new party organs, Apostol was unable to thwart his plans.

THE USE OF POPULISM

Throughout 1966 and 1967 Ceausescu engaged in populist activities to bolster the standing of the party and his own standing as general secretary. During this period of transition, the collective leadership agreed that the support of the people was vital. Wages were increased, the pension system was reformed and the prices for consumer goods were lowered.[8] At the same time, Ceausescu frequently toured the country promoting nationalism with references to great Romanian historical figures such as Stephen the Great and Michael the Brave.[9] Ceausescu linked himself with these historic figures to promote his image as a Romanian nationalist.

Although Ceausescu and others in the collective leadership stressed nationalism as a means of consolidating the party, the concept of nation was very inclusive. The party's early rhetoric focused on uniting ethnic Romanians and ethnic Hungarians into a common Romanian nation. Nationalism provided the regime some measure of real popular support among all ethnic groups. Although Ceausescu eliminated the Hungarian Autonomous Region in 1968, this action was part of a nation-wide territorial reorganization.[10]

Because Ceausescu had been in charge of cadres and organization since the mid-1950s, he had substantial control over the selection of regional party secretaries. Ceausescu replaced regional leaders in order to provide him a base of party support. By 1967, there was a 50% turnover in regional party secretaries. In addition after the December 1967 party conference, these party secretaries assumed the responsibility for local government that had previously been reserved for regional councils.[11] These actions consolidated the party's authority over local government which also consolidated Ceausescu's power over the state. This was a prelude to the end of collective leadership and the separation of party and state.

Nationalism found its fullest expression in foreign policy. Ceausescu and the collective leadership continued Gheorghiu-Dej's policy regarding Comecon economic integration, friendly relations with the Chinese and trade relations with the West. In January 1967, Romania was the first Warsaw Pact country to establish diplomatic relations with West Germany, and later in that year Romania indicated its reluctance to participate in Warsaw Pact maneuvers. These episodes increased the popular support of the PCR and further established Ceausescu's authority. Also during 1966 and 1967, several members of the collective leadership, particularly Apostol, Draghici and Stoica, became less visible both in press reports and in public.[12] By the end of 1967 Ceausescu had established himself as first among equals.

The December 1967 Party Congress enacted several changes to the party's statutes that would eventually assist Ceausescu in gaining complete authority over the party, the state and the population. The Congress enacted territorial reforms and established county party secretaries as heads of local government. This last change was enacted because the 1965 provision restricting an individual from holding joint party and state posts was eliminated. A reorganization of the Central Committee left Stoica without a staff and reassigned Draghici from his party post to a state position in the Council of Ministers. All of these actions were a prelude to the 1968 April Central Committee plenum.

While there was continuity in foreign policy, the collective leadership under Ceausescu wanted to distance itself from the Gheorghiu-Dej legacy. Criticisms of the previous regime made it easier for Ceausescu to replace some long-standing party members, and at the April Central Committee plenum the investigation committee that had been established at the 1965 Party Congress finally issued its report. The committee was charged with examining the circumstances surrounding the removal of PCR members during the Gheorghiu-Dej regime. The committee found that Patrascanu, one of the most important PCR members during the interwar period and early popular front governments, had been unfairly accused of being a spy. The group that made the charges against Patrascanu included Gheorghiu-Dej and Draghici. The Committee maintained that they had usurped the authority of the party, and decided to remove Draghici from all party bodies and recommend that he be removed from his post in the Council of Ministers. Also implicated in the arrest of Patrascanu were Politburo members Apostol and Stoica.[13] By 1968, Ceausescu had successfully eliminated a number of his party rivals.

INVASION OF CZECHOSLOVAKIA

The Romanian response to the Soviet invasion of Czechoslovakia has been described as "the founding myth of Ceausescu's regime."[14] Ceausescu's refusal to provide troops for the Warsaw Pact invasion was a turning point in his leadership. Not only did this event increase his visibility and stature in the West, Ceausescu's denouncement of the invasion of Czechoslovakia also provided him with more legitimacy in Romania. Ceausescu's defiance was considered the ultimate expression of nationalism. Similar to Gheorghiu-Dej during the early 1960s, Ceausescu used foreign policy to mobilize his domestic constituency.

Romania's refusal to participate in the invasion was anticipated by the member-states of the Warsaw Pact. The invasion in August 1968 had been preceded by a series of Warsaw Pact meetings in March, July and August, and Romania was not invited to the discussions.[15] In fact shortly before the invasion, Ceausescu had signed a treaty of friendship with Dubcek in Prague. In a graduating speech at the Bucharest Military Academy on 14 August, Ceausescu stated that nothing could "justify the use of armed force to intervene in the internal affairs of a member country of the Warsaw Pact."[16] During the period of the invasion, Ceausescu continued denouncing the Soviet actions. In a speech delivered in Bucharest on 21 August, he stated that the invasion was a "great error and a serious danger."[17] In response to these statements, several communist party newspapers, including the Hungarian *Magyar Hirlap*, accused Ceausescu of overt nationalism. Because of the statements coming from Budapest and a concern over the reaction of Romania's ethnic Hungarians, Ceausescu decided to stop denouncing the invasion and instead tour Romanian counties that had a substantial Hungarian population.[18] The predominantly ethnic Hungarian counties of Harghita and Covasna subsequently received higher levels of investment in the last years of the Fourth Five-Year Plan, and Ceausescu created a National Council for both ethnic Hungarians and ethnic Germans that would address minority problems. He wanted to ensure that the country's ethnic minorities did not use the invasion as a pretext to press for a change in the party's leadership.

Between 1968 and 1970, Ceausescu continued his populist message. In economic matters, he urged a reduction in wage inequalities; although, the Fifth Five-Year Plan (1971–1975) adopted at the Tenth Party Congress in 1969 continued the policy of industrialization without seriously addressing the standard of living.[19] In cultural matters, he allowed a diversity of opinion (albeit with party supervision). Even in the party, Ceausescu promoted new statutes that allowed members to appeal the decision of the majority (violating the principle of democratic centralism). Although he supposedly was encouraging more discussion within the party, Ceausescu ensured that his position in the party hierarchy was unassailable. By the time of the Tenth Party Congress, Ceausescu had successfully replaced many members of the Political Bureau Executive Committee and the Secretariat.[20] Ceausescu's denouncement of the Warsaw Pact invasion increased his international prestige. President Nixon visited Romania in the summer of 1969. This was first time that an American president had visited a Warsaw Pact country. Ceausescu used nationalist slogans, populist appeals and party appointments to consolidate his position, and by 1969 the period of collective leadership had ended. With his position secure, Ceausescu began to construct his cult of personality.

THE ORIGINS OF CEAUSESCU'S SULTANISTIC REGIME

Juan Linz and Alfred Stepan argue that Ceausescu's cult of personality and regime were unlike those developed by Mao or Stalin. Using Max Weber's concept of sultanism, they argue that Ceausescu's regime was neither authoritarian nor totalitarian.[21] Instead, the regime was extremely patrimonial, characterized by a fusion of public and private spheres, lack of impersonal ideology, dynastic succession and most of all unchecked authority.[22] Ceausescu's need to create a sultanistic regime was partially motivated by his failure to define himself as an authentic leader.[23] While he had genuine popularity after the Soviet invasion of Czechoslovakia, he did not develop either the ideas or charisma that would build long-lasting popular support.

As general secretary, Ceausescu used the party to develop his image of a new nation. The cult of personality and sultanistic regime were not only a by-product of his character but were also developed for political and economic reasons. Complete loyalty to Ceausescu ensured that the party and military would not pose a threat to his leadership. Also, the nationalist character of his cult was used to justify the economic demands of the Fifth Five-Year Plan and Sixth

Five-Year Plan (1976–1980). Ceausescu's liberal rhetoric of the 1960s was soon replaced with attacks on intellectuals, journalists, teachers and anyone else involved in mass culture. Romania's "little cultural revolution" started in earnest in 1971 following Ceausescu's visit to China, Vietnam and North Korea and culminated in the "July theses" in which Ceausescu denounced intellectual cosmopolitanism and demanded greater ideological purity. Ceausescu implemented a policy of re-education, stressing nationalism and a vision of himself as the defender of Romanian values.

The cult of personality and sultanistic regime that developed throughout the 1970s had three essential characteristics. Firstly, Ceausescu instituted a policy of elite rotation that he used within the party, the government and the military.[24] Although the principle was never formalized, elites were periodically reassigned to new state or party positions, including a rotation between the national and the county level.[25] This policy ensured that no individual could consolidate power within the party or at the local level. The policy created insecurity among the party elite and thwarted the development of individual expertise which had an impact on economic policy in the 1980s. Not only were party elites constantly being rotated into new positions, the size of the party also expanded. Between 1969 and 1979, the average annual increase in party membership was over 4.5%.[26] From 1970 through 1980, PCR membership as a percent of the population was the highest of any Eastern European communist party.[27] Ceausescu manipulated the rank-and-file membership as well as the party's upper echelons.

A second characteristic of the cult of personality has been referred to as "dynastic socialism."[28] Similar to the familial regime in North Korea, Ceausescu elevated those within his family, especially his wife Elena and their son Nicu. Elena Ceausescu was elected to the Central Committee in 1972 and later to the Political Executive Committee in 1977. She was in charge of party cadres, the second-highest ranking party position and was also chairperson of the National Council for Science and Technology. She was widely regarded as the second most powerful individual in the country.[29] Nicu Ceausescu and his wife were both full members of the Central Committee, and he was first secretary of the Union of Communist Youth. Ceausescu's nepotism extended beyond his immediate family. Several of his brothers held important government and party posts. Even Elena Ceausescu's brother was made a member of the Central Committee.

A third characteristic of Ceausescu's regime was its personalistic quality. Ceausescu was often described simply as "the leader" or "the ruler" (*conducator*). He was not only idolized as an incarnation of Romanian values and one of the world's greatest diplomats, he was also admired for his "significant contributions" to Marxist doctrine. In fact, the Romanian philosophical dictionary devoted more space to Ceausescu, than to Marx, Engels and Lenin combined, and unfortunately he believed his own propaganda.[30] Both he and Elena personally directed the creation of large-scale economic and scientific programs often with disastrous consequences, such as the razing of historic sections of Bucharest to build the enormous People's Palace.

CEAUSESCUISM IN THE 1970S: TRADE POLICY

Ceausescu's domestic policies in the 1970s focused on increasing industrial output, eliminating cultural and intellectual freedom and suppressing ethnic and religious expression. Throughout this period, Ceausescu maintained a strict Stalinist policy of heavy industrialization and de-emphasized consumer goods production. During the Fifth Five-Year Plan (1971–1975), Romanian industrial output increased faster than any other Warsaw Pact country and its GNP growth was the highest in Europe.[31] During this period, the industrial production of machine equipment and tools more than doubled.[32]

Romania could not rely on the Soviet Union to finance its autarkic economic policies, and Ceausescu turned increasingly to the West for trade and finance. During the 1970s, Romania joined a number of international institutions including the GATT in 1971, the IMF in 1972 and the Group of 77 in 1976. In addition, Ceausescu further extended trade relations with Europe and the United States. In 1973, Romania signed several Western European trade agreements, and in 1975 the country was the first in Eastern European to receive most favored nation trade status (MFN) from the United States. During the period from 1958 to 1975, the country's trade with Comecon members declined from 72% of total trade to 37.5%. At the same time, trade with the West increased from 17% to 38%.[33] Romania's significant economic relations provided necessary access to money from private Western banks. To finance industrial growth, the country amassed a substantial foreign debt. The significant growth rates of the 1970s masked the reality of a declining standard of living. The high rate of industrial investment (estimated at 35–40% of GNP), left few resources for the consumer economy.[34]

A problem with Ceausescu's industrial policy was that it over-produced goods of inferior quality (such as poorly designed machine parts). Ceausescu's industrial policy relied not only on loans from the West, but on stimulating trade relations with LDCs. Trade policy with LDCs was instituted for various reasons. Firstly, these markets did not require goods with Western quality standards. Secondly, marketing goods was less necessary and less expensive than in Europe, and thirdly, these countries could provide Romania with long-term trade agreements for the delivery of raw materials (particularly petroleum) which the country's industrial infrastructure needed. Because of the need for raw materials and new markets, trade with LDCs almost doubled between 1970 and 1975.[35] This trade policy was a reflection of Ceausescu's emphasis on foreign relations with LDCs in the 1970s. He traveled increasingly throughout Africa, Asia and Latin America and actively supported Marxist movements and regimes in countries such as Angola, Cambodia and Cuba.[36]

However by the late 1970s, Romania was becoming more dependent on other countries for its economic needs, and its industrial policy required substantial petroleum resources. Throughout the early 1970s, the country relied on moderate imports of petroleum from Arab states to complement its own domestic production. In 1975, imports supplied 25% of the country's petroleum, but by 1979 imports supplied over 53% of the country's petroleum requirements.[37] The other consequence of this trade policy was the disintegration of agriculture. The emphasis on industrial production was at the expense of investment in agriculture. Although agriculture had been the dominant economic sector even after World War II, collectivization, industrial development and poor planning had drastically reduced its productivity.

CEAUSESCUISM IN THE 1970s: ETHNIC RELATIONS

As the economic situation in Romania declined in the late 1970s, Ceausescu turned increasingly to nationalism to provide his regime with some measure of popularity. Ceausescu's nationalism focused on autonomy from the Soviet Union and assimilation of ethnic Hungarians. In foreign relations, his independent stance against Soviet foreign policy won him praise from the West, including visits from Presidents Nixon and Ford. In the domestic sphere, Ceausescu tapped into an anti-Russian sentiment that was prevalent among the population. Like Gheorghiu-Dej, Ceausescu decided that place names should be de-Russified, and historians were allowed to examine the origins of Soviet Moldavia (Bessarabia).[38]

Nationalism was also directed at the country's ethnic minorities, particularly ethnic Hungarians and, to a much lesser extent, ethnic Germans. Ethnic Hungarians constituted approximately 8% of the population, and in the 1970s, the regime supported the efforts of historians that argued that the Geto-Dacian civilization (Romania's ancestor) predated the influx of Hungarian and Slavic tribes.[39] This was perceived by minorities as "an attempt to deny them historical rights of their own, and to lower them to the position of merely tolerated."[40] Throughout the 1970s, Ceausescu continued the policy of induced ethnic assimilation, and because of his industrial policy, the 1973 education law made technical training the priority of the education system. However, very few technical manuals were translated into other languages and so ethnic Hungarian and ethnic German parents were forced to send their children to Romanian language schools if they wanted them to receive a technical education.[41] Minority language instruction at the university level was also discouraged and extremely limited. A policy instituted in the 1970s assigned university graduates to jobs, and this policy resulted in an influx of ethnic Romanians into Transylvania and the assignment of ethnic Hungarians to largely ethnic Romanian areas.[42] Romanian nationalism portrayed the Hungarian government in Budapest as a Russian surrogate that promoted the elimination of Romanian culture and desired the reincorporation of Transylvania into the Hungarian state. While Hungary never recognized Romania's historic claim to Transylvania, the Romanian statements were designed to appeal to the most base ethnic Romanian prejudices.

CEAUSESCUISM IN THE 1970s: INTELLECTUAL EXPRESSION

Although ethnic Hungarian intellectuals were particularly targeted by Ceausescu's nationalist policy, cultural expression by ethnic Romanian intellectuals was also severely limited. The Romanian cultural revolution that Ceausescu instituted in 1971 curtailed intellectual and religious dissent, and he used his personality cult and the *securitate* to enforce this. In their examination of Eastern European dissident movements, Juan Linz and Alfred Stepan conclude that in Romania "the leaders were poets, literary critics, and philosophers, all of whom spoke a deeply encoded language of dissent but none of whom were nationally known organizers of any form of public resistance ... In no country was the penetration by, and fear of, the ruler and his security services so intense."[43]

Two events in 1977 demonstrated that public dissent would be harshly treated by the regime. Between January and March 1977, the Romanian writer and dissident Paul Goma wrote a number of letters concerning human rights abuses that were made public on Radio Free Europe. In January, Goma made public a letter of support for the Czechoslovakian dissident movement Charter '77. In February, he wrote a letter to Ceausescu urging him to support Charter '77 as he had supported the Dubcek regime earlier in 1968. Finally in March, Goma sent a letter to the Helsinki committee demanding the implementation of human rights that were enshrined in the Romanian constitution.[44] The regime acted swiftly and arrested Goma in April 1977 and later exiled him. Also in 1977, miners in the Jiu Valley protested their low wages and went on strike. Ceausescu personally interceded and promised to redress their grievances, but the two leaders of the strike later died under mysterious circumstances. The lessons that these two events taught dissidents was that any public deviation from the regime would not be tolerated. In fact as the economic situation in the country grew worse in the 1980s, Ceausescu's personality cult and irrational planning took on even greater dimensions.

CEAUSESCUISM IN THE 1980s: ECONOMIC AUSTERITY

Throughout the 1970s, the economy seemed to prosper. During the 1973–1974 oil crisis, Romanian exports of refined petroleum products provided the hard currency earnings necessary for the import of crude oil. Ceausescu used these earnings to obtain loans from private Western banks in order to continue his policy of industrialization, but by the late 1970s revenues from refined products were not increasing at the same rate as crude oil imports, and by 1981 the economy faced productivity losses and a mounting debt. He implemented austerity measures to repay the almost US$10 billion of foreign debt. Ceausescu was convinced that the debt was a threat to the country's economic autonomy and ultimately political autonomy. The austerity policy was begun in 1981 and continued throughout the 1980s. The austerity measures included the rationing of heat, gas, food and medical care. Romania heavily exported agricultural goods and other foodstuffs that were normally part of the domestic economy in order to generate hard currency to pay off the debt. This austerity policy dramatically decreased living standards, social welfare and medical care and increased malnutrition, AIDS and infant mortality (by the late 1980s, the country had one of the highest European infant mortality rates).

CEAUSESCUISM IN THE 1980s: ENVIRONMENTAL DESTRUCTION

The environmental impact of the austerity measures was equally disastrous. In order to continue industrial production, brown coal was used in many factories. The pollutants were indiscriminately emitted into the air and the water supply. Between 1972 and 1982, Romania experienced the largest European increase in per capita emissions of sulfur dioxide. During the 1980s, brown coal and lignite production increased over 100%. Also during this period water contamination exceeded purification plant capacity. Of the 2,767 pretreatment and treatment plants, 844 were operating below standard, and sixty-eight plants were inoperable. In addition, 1,364 miles of rivers were polluted and less than 20% of the main waterways provided drinkable water.[45] While there was environmental legislation (the Environmental Protection Law was passed in 1973), the legislation was never enforced. To increase the capacity of industrial production, Ceausescu proposed the creation of a nuclear facility at Cernavoda. This project was begun in 1978 and was so poorly built that his Canadian partners blocked attempts to place the reactor on-line. Perhaps the most infamous environmental legacy of the Ceausescu period was the carbon processing plant at Copsa Mica. With the assistance of a British company, the processing capacity of the plant was expanded to such an extent that it dumped thousands of tons of soot into the air. Everything in and surrounding this Transylvanian city was encased in black carbon. Copsa Mica was emblematic of the communist industrial legacy.

CEAUSESCUISM IN THE 1980s: ETHNICITY AND FOREIGN RELATIONS

By the late 1980s, Ceausescu's relationship with the West had substantially deteriorated due to his economic, political and ethnic minority policies. Throughout the 1980s, he continued his policy of ethnic assimilation into a common Romanian nation. However, he integrated his ethnic and economic policy. Under Ceausescu's personal directive, the regime undertook a policy of "systematization" in which entire villages were razed to create a more "efficient" economy. As part of this policy, he announced a plan in 1988 that would have razed approximately 6,000 villages, particularly in areas containing ethnic Hungarian communities. The policy drew heavy criticism from

Hungary, Western Europe and the United States. American-Romanian relations became so strained over the issue that Ceausescu unilaterally ended the country's MFN status in 1988. Congress had been considering imposing conditions on the further extension of MFN that would have specifically protected the rights of ethnic Hungarians. In addition, Ceausescu's denouncement of Gorbachev's policies of *perestroika* and *glasnost* demonstrated just how isolated he and the PCR had become from other communist leaderships. Ceausescu referred to *perestroika* as a "right-wing deviation" within the communist bloc.

CEAUSESCUISM IN THE 1980s: SOCIETY AND THE YEAR 1989

The combination of political repression, economic austerity and ethnic assimilation produced "desocialization," perhaps one of the most important legacies of the Ceausescu regime. Public and private citizens became detached from the ruling elite (narrowly defined by the end of the 1980s as Ceausescu's family). Although there was a growing sense of frustration within society, there was no organized opposition that could function as a conduit and provide the basis for political reform. As Juan Linz and Alfred Stepan note, unlike Poland and the Solidarity movement or Czechoslovakia and Charter '77, Romania had no organized opposition.[46] Moreover, the personal politics of Ceausescu had isolated him not only from the public but also from the party and the military. His policy of rotation had ultimately alienated the party elites and the rank-and-file from the ruling leadership. Ceausescu's circulation of party members, extreme nepotism and co-option of the military was resented among party members. By stifling reform both within and outside the party, he had sown the seeds for his own demise. In essence, he had removed all the political alternatives to violence.

The economic, political and environmental situation in Romania by late 1989 had severely deteriorated. During November and December 1989, the communist regimes in East Germany, Hungary and Czechoslovakia were repudiated and relinquished power. Unlike Honecker in East Germany or Husak in Czechoslovakia, Ceausescu refused to step down. He became a prisoner of his own cult of personality. He did not recognize the illegitimacy of his regime, his leadership and the position of his family. Because of his inability to recognize the importance of the events of 1989, the Romanian revolution was the most violent transition in Eastern Europe.

The revolution in December of 1989 was the end of a process that had begun earlier in the year. There were very visible signs in early

1989 that the regime was out of touch with the growing feeling of despair felt by the population and many party members. In March 1989, six party veterans circulated an open letter criticizing Ceausescu's economic policies. Two of the signatories, Constantin Parvulescu and Apostol, had been high ranking party members. This incident indicated the level of frustration felt among the *nomenklatura*. In November 1989, the Fourteenth Congress of the PCR re-elected Ceausescu general secretary. He took this opportunity to denounce events in other Eastern European countries and to proclaim the country's adherence to traditional Marxist-Leninist principles. At this time, the public knew of the changes that were occurring in Hungary and more importantly in Bulgaria and Czechoslovakia. The events of the Congress demonstrated "how much Ceausescu and his clique had lost touch with reality. They could not grasp the magnitude of the social crisis in Romania and failed to realize the effect on the Romanians of the revolutionary events in the other Eastern European countries."[47] Moreover, because Ceausescu was the center of public life, all discontent and frustration became centered on him. As Trond Gilberg states, "there was no bond between the ruler and the ruled, merely despair and a deep-seated hatred ready to flare at the earliest opportunity. Ironically, the Romanian population was ultimately united when this despair and hatred could be focused upon a common enemy."[48]

The social crisis erupted on 17 December, when thousands of ethnic Romanians and ethnic Hungarians entered the streets of the city of Timisoara protesting the attempt by the police to evict Pastor Laszlo Tokes from his parish house. Tokes was a priest in the Reformed Church, which served the ethnic-Hungarian community in Timisoara. Because of his outspoken view regarding the systematization plan, he was ordered transferred to a village in another county. His eviction date was set for 15 December 1989, but Tokes refused to leave his parish. Several hundred ethnic Hungarians began to congregate around the church building. Ethnic Romanians joined the candlelight vigils, which were transformed into an anticommunist demonstration. Within just a couple of days, thousands had joined the protests, and troops from the Ministry of the Interior were ordered to violently disperse the crowd. The brutal clashes between unarmed civilians and the security forces in Timisoara was the "threshold of violent conflict" in the Romanian revolution and the eviction of Pastor Tokes was the triggering event. The security forces could have effectively dealt with the population had it not been mobilized. The efforts of Pastor Tokes to engage the population in Timisoara to challenge the government was an important factor in the revolution spreading from city to city.[49] Also, the military refused to fire on civilians, demonstrating that Ceausescu had alienated this important institution.

To bolster support, Ceausescu organized a rally on 21 December in Bucharest, but the rally turned into an anti-Ceausescu demonstration. Protestors soon seized the state television station and many were involved in the formation of the National Salvation Front (*Frontul Salvarii Nationale* or FSN). The FSN was initially composed of communist cadres, student and human rights activists. Ceausescu and his wife attempted to escape but were captured and executed on Christmas Day 1989. While Ceausescu was successful at mobilizing national resources, he was not successful at dealing with the consequences of this mass mobilization. He was unable to maintain elite support. Party elites had been dependent on him for their position and privileges, but by making them dependent upon him and his family, Ceausescu had alienated them. He had eliminated any other option but revolution.

A ROMANIAN REVOLUTION?

Even now, there is no agreement as to whether Romania experienced a revolution or a coup. Many individuals question whether the country experienced a genuine revolution. Some Romanian and Western writers note that the Romanian post-revolutionary leadership consisted mostly of former communists and therefore that the country experienced a coup. Moreover, these writers argue that until 1996 there was no fundamental change in the country's political or social policy. However, revolutionary change should be judged from a country-specific perspective.

Gilberg points out that *communists* and not the communist *party* exerted influence immediately after the revolution.[50] This is an important distinction when one considers that in the short term many post-communist technocrats were members of the party. Communist political leadership was, therefore, not in and of itself an indication of a failed revolution or a coup. What might seem like incremental change from a Western perspective is fundamental change from a Romanian perspective, and herein lies the debate. Some argue that revolutions are rapid with no incremental change. This, however, is an inaccurate view of revolution. All revolutions have a period of rapid change followed by incremental consolidation.[51] For example, it took almost six years after the Russian revolution before the Bolsheviks finally consolidated their power. While the movement towards a market economy and a genuine democracy has been incremental, the political environment of the country has fundamentally changed.

Katherine Verdery and Gail Klingman argue that some form of popular uprising was necessary to end the Ceausescu regime.[52] They believe that a coup alone would not have overthrown him. Others, such as Juilana Geran Pilon, argue that a coup succeeded in hijacking" the revolution.[53] The debate rages in both the West and in Romania. A Romanian survey found remarkable consistency in the way that the population viewed the revolution. Among respondents, only 50% believed that the events in December 1989 were a revolution. Approximately 30% of respondents believed that the events were a coup and 24% believed that the events were carried out by foreigners.[54] This is the unfortunate legacy of the revolution. It was a defining moment in Romanian history, and yet Romanians and Westerners alike interpret the moment in very different fashions.

CONCLUSION

The nationalist elements of the Ceausescu regime continued a well-defined tradition of mass control and Soviet repudiation that started during the later years of the Gheorghiu-Dej regime. Some of the policies of the Ceausescu regime were simply a continuation of previous policies, but Ceausescu's personality cult or sultanistic regime was far beyond what was established by Gheorghiu-Dej. Ceausescu emerged from a period of collective leadership to become the most oppressive Eastern European leader. The lack of debate, economic austerity and the alienation of the party, the military and the public were all factors that contributed to the revolution.[55]

The importance of the revolution is not only that it continued the country's uniqueness in Eastern Europe (every other 1989 transition had been peaceful), but that it had an important influence on the type of democratic transition that the country experienced. The FSN used the revolution in 1990 to garner popular support in the first postcommunist election. Moreover as surveys suggest, there is no consensus on the origins of the revolution. The psychological healing that was necessary following the revolution never occurred. The debate over the release of *securitate* files and accusations against government officials for involvement in the organization illustrate that Ceausescu's legacy and fifty years of communist rule have left a mark on the population that cannot easily be erased.

One of the reasons why the Romanian revolution is unfinished is because of the disagreement over whether the country experienced a genuine revolution. The creation of a civil society is founded on public agreement about fundamental principles. One of these principles is that conflict should not be resolved through the use of force. Unfortunately, violence is one of the defining characteristics of a revolution, but coups generally do not entail public violence and death. For many Romanians the events of 1989 were a coup, and the associated violence was unnecessary. The lesson from 1989 is that violence, whether necessary or not, is a primary way in which to resolve conflict. This belief among some continues to undermine the establishment of a civil society. The lack of civility in society is part of the unfinished revolution.

1   Some authors such as Stephen Fischer-Galati argue that Gheorghiu-Dej had designated Ceausescu his successor in the late 1950s. The succession struggle and the need for collective leadership until 1967 indicate that no individual was viewed within the party as Gheorghiu-Dej's heir-apparent. See, Stephen Fischer-Galati, *20th Century Rumania*, 2nd ed. (New York: Columbia University Press, 1991), p. 184.

2   Maurer was first named president of the Council of Ministers in March 1961. See, Stelian Neagoe, *Istoria Guvernelor Romaniei* (Bucharest: Editura Machiavelli, 1995), pp. 181–184. For a discussion of the responsibilities of the various state organs see, Richard F. Staar, *Communist Regimes in Eastern Europe*, 3rd ed. (Stanford, CA: Hoover Institution Press, 1977), pp. 155–160.

3   Mary Ellen Fischer, *Nicolae Ceausescu: A Study in Political Leadership* (Boulder, CO: Lynne Reinner), p. 71.

4   Article 3 of the constitution states that "In the Romanian Socialist Republic, the leading political force in the integration of society is the Romanian Communist Party." See, *Constitutiile Romane* (Bucharest: Monitorul Oficial, 1993), p. 165.

5   Beria was head of the Ministry of Internal Affairs immediately after Stalin's death. Because of his control of the secret police, other potential successors including Khrushchev and Malenkov distrusted him. Khrushchev quickly acted to remove Beria from important party posts. Michael Shafir, *Romania: Politics, Economics and Society* (Boulder, CO: Lynne Reinner, 1985), p. 70.

6   Vladimir Tismaneanu, "Ceausescu's Socialism," *Problems of Communism*, January/February 1985, p. 60.

7   Mary Ellen Fischer, *Nicolae Ceausescu: A Study in Political Leadership*, pp. 76–82.

8   Ibid, p. 89.

9   Stephen the Great (1457–1504) united the territories of Wallacia and Moldavia against Turkish rule, and Michael the Brave (1558–1601) temporarily united Wallacia, Moldavia and Transylvania.

10   Trond Gilberg argues that this change began a policy of ethnic chauvinism. Ethnic Romanians replaced ethnic Hungarians in important regional party posts. However, it is unclear whether these changes were motivated by ethnic concerns or simply because these individuals supported Ceausescu. These replacements were necessary to consolidate his power at the regional level rather than to assail ethnic Hungarians. However by the later 1970s and throughout the 1980s,

Ceausescu engaged in discriminatory ethnic policies. See, Trond Gilberg, *Nationalism and Communism in Romania: The Rise and Fall of Ceausescu's Personal Dictatorship* (Boulder, CO: Westview Press, 1991), p. 174.

11   Michael Shafir, *Romania: Politics, Economics and Society*, p. 73.

12   Mary Ellen Fischer, *Nicolae Ceausescu: A Study in Political Leadership*, pp. 106-108.

13   Ibid, p. 132.

14   Gabriel Ivan, "1968, Azi," *Sfera politicii*, July–August 1993, p. 8.

15   Robin Alison Remington, *Winter in Prague Spring: Documents on Czechoslovak Communism in Crisis* (Cambridge, MA: M.I.T. Press, 1969), p. 58.

16   As quoted in, George Cioaranescu, "Rumania After Czechoslovakia: Ceausescu Walks the Tightrope," *East Europe*, June 1969, p. 2.

17   Robin Alison Remington, *Winter in Prague Spring: Documents on Czechoslovak Communism in Crisis*, p. 359.

18   Dennis Deletant, *Romania sub regimul comunist* (Bucharest: Civic Academy Foundation, 1997), pp. 130-131.

19   Michael Cismarescu, "Rumania's Industrial Development," *East Europe*, January 1970, p. 6.

20   Mary Ellen Fischer, *Nicolae Ceausescu: A Study in Political Leadership*, p. 157.

21   Juan J. Linz and Alfred Stepan, *Problems of Democratic Transition and Consolidation: Southern Europe, South America, and Post-Communist Europe* (Baltimore, MD: The Johns Hopkins University Press, 1996), pp. 349-356.

22   Ibid, p. 52.

23   Fischer argues that rather than becoming an authentic leader, Ceausescu wanted to become an idol. See, Mary Ellen Fischer, *Nicolae Ceausescu: A Study in Political Leadership*, pp. 160-165.

24   Not only was the military restructured, Ceausescu also developed a parallel organization called the Patriotic Guard that was completely controlled by the party. See, William Crowther, "'Ceausescuism' and Civil-Military Relations in Romania," *Armed Forces and Society*, Winter 1989, pp. 207-225.

25   Michael Shafir, *Romania: Politics, Economics and Society*, p. 73.

26   This figure was calculated from data collected by Mary Ellen Fischer. See, Mary Ellen Fischer, "The Romanian Communist Party and Its Central Committee: Patterns of Growth and Change," *Southeastern Europe*, January 1979, p. 23.

27   Michael Shafir, *Romania: Politics, Economics and Society*, p. 86.

28   Vladimir Tismaneanu, "Ceausescu's Socialism," p. 62.

29   Walter M. Bacon, Jr., "Romania: Neo-Stalinism in Search of Legitimacy," *Current History*, April 1981, p. 172.

30   Vladimir Tismaneanu, "Ceausescu's Socialism," p. 63.

31   Daniel N. Nelson, "Romania," in Zoltan Barany and Ivan Volgyes, eds., *The Legacies of Communism in Eastern Europe* (Baltimore, MD: The Johns Hopkins University Press, 1995), p. 199.

32   Dan Sava, "Progresul technic-factor de baza in dezvoltarea intensiva a industriei," *Revista economica*, December 1985, p. 16.

33   Robert L. Farlow, "Romania: The Politics of Autonomy," *Current History*, April 1978, p. 170.

34   Daniel N. Nelson, "Romania," p. 203.

35   Robert R. King, "Romania and the Third World," *Orbis*, Winter 1978, p. 875.

36   Trond Gilberg, *Nationalism and Communism in Romania: The Rise and Fall of Ceausescu's Personal Dictatorship*, pp. 218-220.

37   These figures were calculated from data collected by Michael Shafir. See, Michael Shafir, *Romania: Politics, Economics and Society*, p. 111.

38   Walter M. Bacon, Jr., "Romania: Neo-Stalinism in Search of Legitimacy," p. 171.

39   The percentage of ethnic Germans declined in the 1970s to 1.6% because Ceausescu allowed many to immigrate to West Germany.

40   Michael Shafir, *Romania: Politics, Economics and Society*, pp. 159-160.

41   Ibid, p. 163.

42   Mary Ellen Fischer, *Nicolae Ceausescu: A Study in Political Leadership*, pp. 245-246.

43 Juan J. Linz and Alfred Stepan, *Problems of Democratic Transition and Consolidation: Southern Europe, South America, and Post-Communist Europe*, pp. 353–354.

44 Michael Shafir, *Romania: Politics, Economics and Society*, pp. 170.

45 Edward Maitland, "Romania's Environmental Crisis," in Joan DeBardeleben, ed., *To Breathe Free* (Washington D.C.: Woodrow Wilson Center, 1991), pp. 235–236.

46 Juan J. Linz and Alfred Stepan, *Problems of Democratic Transition and Consolidation: Southern Europe, South America, and Post-Communist Europe*, pp. 352–354.

47 Vladimir Tismaneanu, "The Revival of Politics in Romania," in Nils H. Wessell, ed., *The New Europe: Revolution in East-West Relations* (New York: The Academy of Political Science, 1991), p. 89.

48 Trond Gilberg, *Nationalism and Communism in Romania: The Rise and Fall of Ceausescu's Personal Dictatorship*, p. 270.

49 Vladimir Socor, "Pastor Tokes and the Outbreak of the Revolution in Timisoara," *RFE: Report on Eastern Europe*, 2 February, 1990, pp. 19–26.

50 Trond Gilberg, *Nationalism and Communism in Romania: The Rise and Fall of Ceausescu's Personal Dictatorship*, p. 278.

51 For an application of revolutionary theory to the Romanian case see, Steven D. Roper, "The Romanian Revolution from a Theoretical Perspective," *Communist and Post Communist Studies*, December 1994, pp. 401–410.

52 Katherine Verdery and Gail Klingman, "Romania after Ceausescu: Post-Communist Communism?," in Ivo Banac, ed., *Eastern Europe in Revolution* (Ithaca, NY: Cornell University Press, 1992), p. 121.

53 Juliana Geran Pilon, *The Bloody Flag: Post-Communist Nationalism in Eastern Europe* (New Brunswick, NJ: Transaction Publishers, 1992), p. 4.

54 Pavel Campeanu, "Sondaje de decembrie: Decembrie '89 versiunea lui decembrie '95," 22, January 1996, p. 7.

55 The exact number of deaths during the revolution is still disputed. Initially, there were claims that 60,000 persons had died. These figures were later significantly modified. The correct number is between 1,000 and 2,000.

Chapter 4

ROMANIAN POLITICAL DEVELOPMENT: 1990–1999

Following the execution of Nicolae and Elena Ceausescu, the FSN developed from a movement into a party. Because of its leading role during the events of December 1989, the FSN established the parameters in which institutional decisions were made. The FSN was responsible for organizing the first government and establishing the first electoral system. As a consequence between 1990 and 1996, the FSN, or some variant of the party, fundamentally influenced the process of democratization and economic reform. Indeed many critics argue that some of the leaders of the original FSN, most notably Iliescu, are largely responsible for the current lack of civil society and economic reform.

During the 1996 parliamentary and presidential election, the opposition blamed the government for allowing Romania to fall economically behind Poland, the Czech Republic and Hungary. Romania, which had always had a more pro-Western orientation during the communist period until 1980, was now seen by many as antireformist and antidemocratic. The opposition that won the 1996 elections inherited a political system plagued by political corruption and an economic crisis. Since 1996, the country has attempted to implement necessary economic reforms; however, infighting within the government coalition has caused political and economic instability. To understand the problems that Romania confronts, it is important to examine the development of the political system since 1990. This chapter examines the development of the party system and explores the issues that have influenced the process of democratization.

THE ESTABLISHMENT OF THE FSN

In a radio and television address on 22 December 1989, Iliescu, a prominent member of the PCR before his demotion in 1971, announced that the "Ceausescu clan which has destroyed the country has been eliminated from power."[1] At that moment, he announced the creation of the FSN. Within four days, the FSN formed a provisional government with Petre Roman as prime minister, and Iliescu as president of the FSN Council and interim president of the country. The original members of the FSN Council included intellectuals, army officers and students, but the most prominent members were former communist officials. Within just a few weeks, many of the important FSN Council intellectuals quit the organization.

On 27 December, the Council issued a directive abolishing the hegemonic position of the PCR and guaranteeing future elections. At first the FSN claimed that it was not a party and that it would not nominate candidates for the upcoming elections. However in January, the FSN issued a statement declaring its intentions to participate in the elections, and on 6 February 1990 it became the twenty-seventh party formally registered to compete in the April national elections.[2] Public opinion polls showed that almost 82% of respondents agreed with the FSN's decision to register.[3] At that time, the FSN enjoyed widespread support because of its role in December 1989 and its control over the mass media, particularly television.

In contrast, the leaders of the three historic interwar parties of Romania, the PNL, the PSDR, and the renamed National Peasants Party Christian Democratic (*Partidul National Taranesc Crestin Democrat* or PNTCD) protested the decision of the FSN. They argued that there could not be fair elections if the FSN both organized and participated in the elections, and the FSN Council agreed to hold discussions with leaders from the various parties to dispel any perception that it was monopolizing power.

As a consequence of these discussions, a Provisional Council of National Unity was formed. The Council became the *de facto* parliamentary body until the elections. Approximately 50% of the Council's membership came from the FSN, and the other 50% was drawn from the other registered parties. On 14 March, the Council issued a decree that postponed the elections from April until 20 May. The decree mandated the creation of a bicameral parliament comprised of a lower house (Assembly of Deputies) and an upper house (Senate). This decree also established that the parliament would have eighteen months to ratify a constitution, and that twelve months after the constitution was ratified, new elections had to occur. Although the Council issued the decree, it was clear that the FSN Executive Office and Iliescu were the primary sources of authority.

While Iliescu and the FSN established the political agenda, nationalist ideology became a polarizing force soon after December 1989. Throughout January and February 1990, the revolution was viewed as a political event that had brought ethnic groups together. This view culminated in the Proclamation of Timisoara of 11 March 1990. The leaders of the revolution issued this document to clarify the goals of the revolution. They felt that the revolution was a multiethnic phenomenon and that ethnic minority tolerance and not chauvinism should be the basis of ethnic relations.[4]

Unfortunately less than a week after issuing this document, events demonstrated the precarious nature of ethnic relations. On 15 March, ethnic Hungarians in Transylvanian towns such as Satu Mare, Sovata and Targu Mures celebrated the anniversary of the 1848 Hungarian revolution. These celebrations were interpreted by some as anti-Romanian, and within a few days several ethnic Romanian organizations started demonstrating. Between 15 and 20 March, clashes occurred that left five dead and hundreds injured. These events demonstrated the volatile nature of ethnic relations. Moreover, this incident was used by some nationalist parties, such as the newly formed Party of Romanian National Unity (*Partidul Unitatii Nationale Romane* or PUNR), to attempt to gain an advantage in the forthcoming elections.[5] While these nationalist parties did not perform well in the 1990 national elections, they became much more important throughout the 1990s.

THE 1990 NATIONAL ELECTIONS

In the May 1990 parliamentary election, Romania used a system of proportional representation with closed party lists while the presidential election used a majority run-off system in which a candidate needed an absolute majority in the first round. If no candidate received an absolute majority in the first round, then a second round would be held between the two candidates who received the most first round votes. All of the preelection polls indicated strong support for the FSN, particularly among rural voters and industrial workers. The opposition parties, most notably the PNL and the PNTCD, had the support of intellectuals in urban areas.

Seventy-three parties participated in the parliamentary election; however, FSN candidates received an overwhelming 66% of the popular vote and approximately 68% of the lower house seats (see Table 4.1) and Roman was once again named prime minister. Presidential candidate Iliescu received over 85% of the vote. The success of the FSN in the first postcommunist election was unlike other East European parties. Some scholars argue that the success of the FSN was because of electoral fraud. However, public opinion polls conducted after the 1990 elections found that the overwhelming

TABLE 4.1 1990 PARLIAMENTARY ELECTIONS (ASSEMBLY OF DEPUTIES)

PARTY[a]	VOTE %	NUMBER OF SEATS	SEAT %
National Salvation Front	66.31	263	67.9
Hungarian Democratic Union of Romania	7.23	29	7.5
National Liberal Party	6.41	29	7.5
Romanian Ecological Movement	2.62	12	3.1
National Peasants Party	2.56	12	3.1
Alliance for a United Romania	2.12	9	2.3
Democratic Agrarian Party of Romania	1.83	9	2.3
Romanian Ecological Party	1.69	8	2.1
Romanian Socialist Democratic Party	1.05	5	1.3

Source: Ariadna Combes and Mihnea Berindei, "Analiza alegerilor," in Pavel Campeanu, Ariadna Combes and Mihnea Berindei, eds., Romania inainte si dupa 20 Mai (Bucharest: Humanitas, 1991), pp. 75–76.
[a]Only those parties and organizations that received 1% of the vote were included. Nine other parties received seats in the lower house.

majority of voters believed that the election returns were accurate. In one poll, over 80% of respondents stated that they believed the counting of the ballots was done correctly and over 75% indicated that they were satisfied with the election results.[6]

The FSN's electoral success was due primarily to the lack of any real opposition, the manipulation of the mass media and the violent nature of the country's transition. Ironically the FSN, as a former communist party, benefited the most from Ceausescu's cult of personality and use of the secret police, which undermined any opposition movement or underground media. Because of the cult of personality, frustrations were focused more on the individual (or in this case the family) than on the institution of the party. The FSN could rely on the party's former institutional links, but the apparent success of the FSN in the 1990 elections was deceptive. Because the FSN benefited from Ceausescu's legacy, the party never developed a specific program to appeal to voters. There was no electoral necessity to present a well thought-out and cohesive party platform. It was a broad, catch-all party and never clearly defined its program.

Another consequence of the FSN's electoral success was that the party, and by extension the country, never directly addressed either Romania's communist legacy or the origin of the December revolution. The dominance of the FSN after the first postcommunist elections prevented this type of national discussion from occurring. When the FSN was confronted with its own communist past, the party's reaction was to eliminate any opposition. As an example, in June 1990 Bucharest students assembled at University Square protesting the

Roman government; instead of engaging the students in discussions, the government called on miners from the Jiu Valley to violently disperse the students. Iliescu went so far as to describe the students as "hooligans," a favorite Ceausescu expression. In addition the party suppressed debate by using the newly reconstituted *securitate*, the Romanian Information Service. The head of the service, Virgil Magureanu, was a close associate of Iliescu. As a consequence of the FSN's electoral success, the party and the country never engaged in any serious soul-searching after the events of December 1989.

THE NEW CONSTITUTION

Following the elections, the primary task of the parliament was to draft a new constitution. The composition of the drafting committee reflected the parties' parliamentary strength. The FSN dominated the committee, and the most crucial issue confronting the committee was the distribution of power between the parliament and the executive. President Iliescu and the FSN MPs wanted a strong presidency while other parties were less enthusiastic.

The constitution was overwhelmingly approved by the parliament. Over 81% of MPs voted for it in November 1991 (which was later endorsed in a December referendum). Significantly, however, almost all the members of the Hungarian Democratic Union of Romania (*Uniunea Democrata Maghiara din Romania* or UDMR) and the PNTCD voted against it. The MPs of these parties felt that a specific reference to "separation of powers" should have been included and that the constitution granted too much authority to the executive. The constitution established a "semi-presidential" system based on the French model. Power is shared between the prime minister and the president. Article 102 stipulates that the president and not the parliament nominates the prime minister, and that it is the president who dismisses the prime minister. In addition, Articles 86 and 87 grant the president the right to consult with government and participate in government meetings. The constitution also provides the president emergency powers and the authority to propose referenda. Following the adoption of the constitution by referendum, the next task for the parliament was to organize new national elections.

WAR OF THE ROSES

The FSN had always been a party coalition composed of competing and often contradictory viewpoints. In early 1991, the coalition fragmented around the issue of economic reform. As the parliament debated economic legislation, members became divided over the pace and substance of reform. Two factions emerged centered around Iliescu and Roman. According to the law and as later enshrined in the constitution, Iliescu relinquished his party membership upon taking office. Therefore, Roman was chosen as the party's national leader. The Roman wing of the FSN advocated a faster pace of economic reform than the Iliescu wing. The debate was managed and largely kept within the party until the end of 1991.

In September 1991, the same Jiu Valley miners once again descended on Bucharest. This time the miners did not come to protect the government but to protest against it. They were demonstrating against their declining living standards, and Roman handed in his mandate and offered to reshuffle the cabinet to avert a crisis. Roman did not intend to resign but rather to change the government. Iliescu, however, announced that he had accepted the resignation of the cabinet. Roman protested that he had not resigned but handed in his mandate, but Iliescu dismissed this as a "semantic difference."[7] This semantic difference led to a crisis in the FSN. Members had to choose sides in a battle that the media dubbed the "war of the roses," an allusion to the FSN's rose electoral symbol. From December 1991 through March 1992, the FSN membership engaged in acrimonious debate over the nature of economic reform and the country's communist legacy. Iliescu accused Roman of being "one of those scores of postrevolutionary pork-chop-hunters" while Roman called Iliescu a "crypto-communist."[8] After Roman's dismissal, Iliescu appointed the finance minister, Theodor Stolojan, as the new prime minister.

THE CONSOLIDATION OF THE OPPOSITION AND A SPLIT IN THE FSN

The height of the FSN infighting occurred during the February and March 1992 mayoral, city and county council elections. Not surprisingly, the FSN did not perform well in these local elections because of the party's division and because of a more unified opposition. In November 1991, opposition parties started discussions concerning the formation of an electoral coalition, the Democratic Convention of Romania (*Conventia Democratica din Romania* or CDR). Although many of the members of the coalition have changed since its inception in late 1991, there was a core group of parties in the CDR in 1991 including the Civic Alliance Party (*Partidul Aliantei Civice* or PAC), the Romanian Ecological Party (*Partidul Ecologist Roman* or PER), the PNTCD, the UDMR, the PNL and the PSDR. In addition, several associations and civic organizations joined the coalition including the Civic Alliance and the Association of Former Political Detainees of Romania.

The 1992 local elections were the first elections that the CDR participated in. Local elections were held on five separate dates in February and March. The CDR, the largest opposition coalition, won the mayoral contests in several important cities including Bucharest, Timisoara, Constanta and Brasov. In fact, the CDR won almost 65% of the mayoral contests in municipalities with a population over 200,000. The FSN's significant defeats in major urban areas acerbated the party conflict.

During this period, several factions developed in the FSN. Two of the factions, the Group for the Front's Unity (*Grupul pentru Unitatea Frontului* or GUF) and A Future for Romania (*Viitor pentru Romania* or VR) were closely aligned with Iliescu, while a third faction was aligned with Roman. On 27 March 1992, the FSN held its national convention which only amplified the division between the followers of Iliescu and Roman. Although Iliescu was not formally a party member, he used the GUF and the VR to present his case. On the second day of the convention, the FSN delegates adopted a new party platform for the forthcoming national elections. The Roman faction, the GUF and the VR each presented a draft proposal. This was an important issue because the leader of the group whose program was adopted would automatically be named the national party leader. Both the GUF and the VR drafts insisted that a strong social policy should accompany any market reforms. The Roman faction presented a draft that envisioned the FSN as a center-left party committed to economic reform. Many observers stated that there were no substantial policy differences between these three drafts. Instead of formulating specific policy proposals, most of the debate and attention focused on the selection of the party leader. At the end of the second day of the convention, delegates voted on the drafts. The Roman platform received an absolute majority, and Roman was re-elected party leader.

On the third and final day of the convention, the most important issue involved the forthcoming national elections. The victorious Roman wing refused to consider the nomination of a presidential candidate until the date of the elections had been established. They wanted to hold another convention later in the spring to choose the party's presidential candidate. The Iliescu wing considered this

decision an obvious attempt to embarrass the president. As a consequence, hundreds of Iliescu supporters protested the decision and left
the convention. The next day, several FSN MPs renounced their party
membership (most of the FSN MPs were Iliescu supporters) and
expressed their intention to create a new party. The splintering of the
FSN was an important moment in postcommunist Romania because it
demonstrated clear divisions even among former communists. The
more reform-minded members stayed in the FSN while those that were
less sympathetic to market reform left the party. The splintering of the
FSN occurred just six months before the national elections so it was
imperative for Iliescu supporters to quickly establish a party.

Following the convention, several hundred Iliescu supporters met
on 30 March 1992 to discuss the creation of a committee that would
establish a new party. These supporters were not only former members
of the FSN but also of the PCR and represented much of the old
nomenklatura. Iliescu's supporters decided to name their party the
Democratic National Salvation Front (*Frontul Democrat al Salvarii
Nationale* or FDSN). In June the party held its first national convention which approved a party platform based on populist notions of
social protection. The FDSN portrayed the FSN as elitist and unsympathetic to the plight of workers.

Although the FDSN held no government portfolios, within three
months it established itself as a legitimate party and a contender in the
national elections. By the summer, the FDSN held a majority of seats
in the Senate and over fifty seats in the lower house. In addition,
several FSN county organizations joined the FDSN. At the June
national convention, Oliviu Gherman was elected party president, and
Iliescu was nominated as the FDSN's presidential candidate in a
process described in the media as the "fifteenth PCR congress."[10] The
FDSN's rapid consolidation of power was helped by several important
defections from the FSN at both the national and the local county
level.

THE 1992 NATIONAL ELECTIONS

The FDSN used it support in the parliament to delay the passage of a
new electoral law. The 1992 national elections were initially scheduled for sometime in June or July; however because the electoral law
was passed so late, the elections were postponed until September. The
additional three months assisted the FDSN in establishing itself as a
legitimate and leading party. Unlike the 1990 national elections, the

newly constituted FDSN faced a serious challenge not only from the FSN but also from the opposition CDR, which had won impressive victories in the recent local elections. The FDSN waged a war on two fronts. It blamed the Roman government for the corruption and scandal that was endemic in the country's politics and emphasized its more "moderate" approach to economic development. With regards to the CDR, the FDSN relied on scare tactics, the relative inexperience of CDR candidates as well as the advanced age of many in the leadership. The FDSN warned that, if elected, a CDR government would begin a witch-hunt for former communists. It also argued that the CDR leadership, particularly PNTCD members, were too old to lead the country and that their real agenda was revenge against communist party members. The CDR leadership denied these charges, but the accusations were effective.

During the summer, the CDR was preoccupied with the selection of its presidential nominee. Several individuals had indicated an interest in becoming the nominee, and the selection of a candidate created conflict between the member-parties. Not only did the struggle over the presidential nomination cause friction between parties, the nomination process also caused friction between some of the parties and the CDR associations. While these associations did not field their own candidates, they had a significant influence on the internal structure of the organization. These associations had voting privileges in the selection of the presidential nominee, and they were viewed by many member-parties as instruments of the PNTCD. The leadership selected Emil Constantinescu as their presidential nominee. Constantinescu, rector of the University of Bucharest, was considered an unlikely candidate. However, other candidates had enough enemies in the coalition to block their nominations. Constantinescu never affiliated himself with a specific party, and because of his neutral stance became a compromise nominee who was acceptable to all the parties and the associations.

The FDSN's concern about the strength of the CDR was substantiated by many of the pre-electoral polls. Several polls conducted during the summer found that the CDR would win a plurality, the largest share of the votes, for the parliamentary elections and a significant share of the presidential vote. For example, the last poll published by the Institute for Marketing and Polling predicted that the CDR would receive 29.5% of the parliamentary vote and the FDSN only 12.5%. This poll predicted that the CDR presidential candidate,

Constantinescu, would receive 34% of the vote while Iliescu would receive 27%.

The FDSN, however, was far more successful in the elections than the polls had predicted (see Table 4.2). It received approximately 28% of the vote (approximately 35% of the parliamentary seats) while the CDR won just over 20% of the vote. The FSN only received 10% of the vote. Although the FDSN no longer held an absolute majority in the parliament, it held more seats than any other party. Unlike the 1990 parliamentary elections, the 1992 electoral law stipulated a 3% national threshold. A party had to receive at least 3% of the national vote in order to receive a seat. Because of this threshold, the number of parliamentary parties declined. While eighteen parties and coalitions received seats in the lower house in 1990, only seven parties and coalitions received seats in 1992, including several nationalist parties.[11]

While the pre-electoral polls had accurately predicted that there would be a second round presidential run-off between Iliescu and Constantinescu, they had underestimated voter support for Iliescu. While Iliescu's margin of victory declined in the 1992 presidential election (he received just over 61% of the second round vote), he was re-elected during a time in which other East European incumbents were being defeated. While FDSN opponents argued that this sharp decline in presidential popularity indicated a lack of confidence in Iliescu and his party, supporters argued that the margin of victory reflected a more realistic view of postcommunist politics.

Some in the opposition argued that the FDSN had stolen the election. Over 10% of ballots were nullified because of procedural irregu-

TABLE 4.2   1992 PARLIAMENTARY ELECTIONS (HOUSE OF DEPUTIES)

PARTY[a]	VOTE %	NUMBER OF SEATS	SEAT %
Democratic National Salvation Front (FDSN)	27.71	117	35.7
Democratic Convention of Romania (CDR)	20.01	82	25.0
National Salvation Front (FSN)	10.18	43	13.1
Party of Romanian National Unity (PUNR)	7.71	30	9.1
Hungarian Democratic Union of Romania (UDMR)	7.45	27	8.2
Greater Romania Party (PRM)	3.89	16	4.9
Socialist Labor Party (PSM)	3.03	13	3.4
Total[b]	79.98	328	100.0

Source: Monitorul oficial al Romaniei, 257, 15 October 1992, pp. 2–13.
[a]Includes only those parties and organizations that passed the 3% threshold.
[b]Does not include ethnic-based parties that were awarded a seat per the constitution.

larities (e.g., double-stamping the ballot). However, it was never proven that fraud changed the electoral outcome. Some, such as opposition leader Nicolae Manolescu, publicly declared that "we [the CDR] did not lose because of fraud but because we were unable to convince the Romanian electorate that we were better than the others."[12] Manolescu was partially correct. The CDR did not present a positive message that attracted voters, and as a consequence the FDSN benefited from the opposition's lack of political experience.

However, the FDSN, through Iliescu's influence, obtained significant material and media resources. Firstly, the FDSN was very successful at capturing former FSN county organizations and persuading county prefects (appointed governors) to join the party. One of the reasons why the FSN did so poorly in the elections was because its local electoral base had largely defected to the FDSN. Secondly, Iliescu used his authority over state television (TVR) to influence the reporting on the election. Just before the elections, Iliescu had established a National Audiovisual Council that was responsible for overseeing the media, and the membership of the Council was largely drawn from the FDSN. The party used all of Iliescu's presidential privileges during the election. Less than seven months after its registration, the FDSN had the task of forming a new coalition government.

THE FDSN COALITION GOVERNMENT

Because the FDSN only held a plurality of seats, it brokered agreements with other parties. The composition of the new parliament reflected an increasing polarization in Romanian politics. Unlike the 1990 parliament, there was now a clear opposition, the CDR, and several extremist parties including the Greater Romania Party (*Partidul Romania Mare* or PRM), the Socialist Labor Party (*Partidul Socialist al Muncii* or PSM) and the PUNR. Gheorghe Funar, the controversial Mayor of Cluj, led the PUNR. Corneliu Vadim Tudor, a Ceausescu associate, was the chair of the PRM, and former Ceausescu prime minister Ilie Verdet was the chair of the PSM. All three parties were nationalist and often vehemently anti-Hungarian, anti-Semitic and openly nostalgic for the Ceausescu regime.

The FDSN unofficially and covertly formed a coalition government with these parties. There was no serious negotiation with the opposition CDR and the UDMR refused to participate in a FDSN government. Roman's FSN, which later changed its name to the Democratic Party National Salvation Front (*Partidul Democrat Frontul Salvarii*

Nationale or PD FSN), was also not acceptable. Although the FDSN formed a coalition with these nationalist and leftist parties, FDSN members held almost all the government portfolios, and Iliescu appointed his associate Nicolae Vacariou as the new prime minister. In addition, FDSN member Adrian Nastase was chosen president of the House of Deputies, and FDSN party president Gherman was elected president of the Senate.

Although the composition of the parliament and the government changed, the domination of Iliescu and the presidency continued. Through the constitutional, and at times the extra-constitutional, powers of the presidency, Iliescu exerted a strong influence on appointments, legislation and foreign policy. Even with his substantial constitutional powers, he often used extra-constitutional authority to influence legislation. During the Roman government, he had created a "shadow government" inside the executive branch, and his staff was organized on the basis of government ministries. This shadow government and the inherent weakness of the parliament provided Iliescu with numerous opportunities to subvert parliamentary power.[13]

Even with the support of Iliescu, the Vacariou government encountered a great deal of difficulty, primarily because of its reliance on coalition partners. The FDSN was dependent on these nationalist parties to pass legislation, and much of the difficulty between the coalition members was because of the informal nature of the relationship. For example, while non-parliamentary PUNR members had held cabinet positions since March 1993, they were not allowed to reveal their party affiliation. Iliescu was concerned that an agreement with the PUNR would be perceived negatively in the West. In fact, the desire for a positive Western perception was one of the reasons why the FDSN officially changed its name to the Party of Social Democracy in Romania (*Partidul Democratiei Sociale din Romania* or PDSR) at its July 1993 national convention. The party leadership wanted to be identified with the European social democratic movement.

In August 1993, the PUNR negotiated to formally enter the cabinet. While the PDSR did not want the PUNR formally included in the cabinet, it needed PUNR parliamentary support. Therefore, the PDSR signed an agreement with the PUNR in January 1994; however, the agreement was not announced until August 1994 when the PUNR officially became the junior member of the government coalition. Not only was the PUNR demanding formal cabinet recognition, the PRM was also requesting government portfolios. Both parties wanted to establish an agreement that would require the coordination of policies at the national and the local levels. After months of negotiating, the PDSR finally signed the agreement with the PUNR, the PRM and the PSM in January 1995.

The agreement stated that the four parties would coordinate policies and that decisions would be consensual. In addition, it promised that the four parties would act against any "anti-Romanian manifestations" (a reference demanded by the PRM). The agreement did not guarantee the PRM or the PSM government portfolios. PDSR Executive Chair Nastase stated that the agreement was a political and not a government document. The PRM and the PSM would be offered lower-level government positions rather than portfolios. While the reaction of the opposition to this protocol was predictable, many members of the signatory parties were also dismayed by the alliance. Soon after the protocol was signed, several leading PSM members left the party. These members did not want to be affiliated with the Vacariou government which was seen as corrupt and ineffective.

The agreement was a desperate attempt by the PDSR to create greater cohesion among the coalition members; however throughout 1993 and into 1994, it was clear that the Vacariou government was pursuing unpopular policies. During this period, three separate votes of confidence were taken, and while these votes failed to topple the government, they sent a signal that the parliament was not satisfied. In March 1994, the Vacariou government was reorganized, but the opposition charged that the changes were not substantial and that they were based on Iliescu's rather than Vacariou's recommendation.

By the end of 1995, a failing economy, charges of corruption and infighting among coalition members plagued the PDSR. Efforts at attracting foreign investment were largely unsuccessful because of Romania's lack of economic reform. Iliescu's attempt to incrementally align economic and foreign policy with the West alienated both real reformers and many former communists. In the mid-1990s, the government was oscillating between economic reform and economic populism. While the economy showed signs of improvement in 1993 and 1994, the statistics masked serious problems that became obvious in 1995.

While Iliescu wanted Romanian integration into Western institutions such as NATO and the EU, he had to resolve the question of the relationship with Hungary and the status of Romania's 1.6 million ethnic Hungarians. In August 1995, Iliescu proposed a new three-part document to hasten the signing of a Romanian-Hungarian treaty.[14] The PDSR's coalition partners were opposed to the proposal. Both the PRM and the PSM refused to support it, and in October 1995, Vacariou removed the PRM from the government coalition. Iliescu remained typically ambiguous about the status of the PUNR or the PSM. The PDSR was unable to consolidate power and maintain a cohesive coalition, and it was the inability to consolidate previous gains that lead to the party's decline.

THE SPLINTERING OF THE OPPOSITION

Like the PDSR, the CDR's postelectoral coalition also disintegrated. The CDR did not perform as well as expected in the 1992 elections, and throughout 1993 and 1994, party divisions emerged in the coalition that led to its fragmentation. On 17 February 1995, the CDR Council issued a three-point protocol that called for member-parties to run on joint lists for the forthcoming 1996 local and parliamentary elections, to support the same presidential candidate and insisted that the UDMR state its support for the constitution, including the provision that defines Romania as a "unitary and national state." CDR member parties including the PAC, UDMR, PSDR and the Liberal Party '93 (*Partidul Liberal '93* or PL '93) refused to sign this protocol. CDR President Constantinescu stated that these four parties were "no longer active in the CDR."[15] He gave these parties thirty days to ratify the protocol.

On 18 February, Sergiu Cunescu, president of the PSDR, protested against what he called "the dictatorship of the PNTCD over the other members."[16] On 24 February, Cunescu announced that the PSDR would not sign the CDR protocol, which amounted to the party's withdrawal from the coalition. He favored the creation of a new opposition coalition without the participation of the PNTCD. Shortly thereafter, the PAC and the PL '93 also left the coalition. By the June 1996 local elections, only the National Liberal Party Democratic Convention, the PNTCD and the PER remained in the coalition.

THE 1996 LOCAL ELECTIONS AND THE DECLINE OF THE PDSR

By the summer of 1996, the Romanian political environment had changed considerably. The PDSR's popularity had significantly declined; the main opposition alliance had splintered, and Roman's PD FSN (renamed simply the Democratic Party) formed a coalition with other social democratic parties called the Social Democratic

Union (*Uniunea Social Democrat* or USD). The 1996 local elections were critical because they provided the first indication of voter reaction to these changes.

In the city council elections, the CDR received 19.6% of the seats, the PDSR received 18.8% and the USD received 12.2%. In mayoral contests, the PDSR received 928 mayoral mandates, the USD received 475 and the CDR received 355. Similar to the 1992 local elections, most of the PDSR mayoral mandates came from small towns and villages and not from major urban areas. However unlike previous elections, voter turnout was low. In the 2 June first round elections, turnout was only 56.5%, and was below 50% for the 16 June second round. The PDSR used the low turnout to justify its performance. When asked about the PDSR's mediocre showing in large cities, Nastase argued that "in the very large localities, very few voted in the local elections and many more will vote in the parliamentary election."[17] He implied that because of the low turnout for the local elections, the results were not important and that the PDSR would perform much better in the national elections. For the CDR, however, the results were significant. The splintering of the coalition had not been detrimental. In fact the fragmenting of the CDR had assisted the coalition in overcoming some of its internal divisions and provided the it with success in the 1996 local elections.

THE 1996 NATIONAL ELECTIONS

The June 1996 local elections, however, sent a clear signal to the PDSR that the party was in trouble. The party's poor performance combined with a further deterioration of the economy throughout the fall, forced Iliescu and the Vacariou government to re-evaluate policies. In September the government was reshuffled, and Iliescu finally signed the basic treaty with Hungary. As a result of the treaty negotiations the PDSR terminated its coalition with the PUNR, thus finally ending the so-called "red quadrangle coalition." Under Funar's leadership, the PUNR became divided by internal conflicts and was no longer an important coalition partner. A number of key PUNR members had resigned during the year.

The disintegration of the PUNR was just one of the changes in Romania's political environment since 1992. There were other changes that greatly affected the outcome of the 1996 election. Firstly, the PDSR no longer controlled the electronic media as it had in 1992. The independent and very popular television station Pro-TV insured that the opposition received equal news coverage. This was important because the PDSR still dominated state television. Secondly, the opposition itself had matured and changed its message. Rather than relying on anticommunist themes, the CDR adopted a more positive "Contract with Romania" which described the problems a CDR government would solve. The 1996 campaign demonstrated that CDR presidential candidate Constantinescu had also matured as a campaigner and a leader. Thirdly, there was a change in the electorate itself. The emerging entrepreneurial class distrusted the PDSR's economic policy, and other economic classes changed their party allegiance because of the poor economic performance of the Vacariou government.

Polls conducted by the Romanian Public Opinion Survey Institute (IRSOP) indicated that many voters approved of the Contract. Approximately 68% of respondents indicated that they had a "very good" or "good" opinion of the CDR's program. While the opposition focused on a positive, substantive message, the PDSR presented its same negative 1992 message, but it did not resonate with the 1996 electorate. In October, another IRSOP poll indicated a reduction in PDSR support. This poll reported that the PDSR vote share had declined from 31% in September to 24%, while the CDR had increased its share to over 30%. Not only were polls showing an increase in support for the CDR, the same polls reported strong support for Roman's USD. As the PDSR became more desperate, its message turned increasingly negative and nationalist.

The results of the parliamentary and presidential election indicated a rejection of the PDSR's negative message (see Table 4.3). The CDR received a plurality of votes in both houses (30%) and formed a coali-

TABLE 4.3   1996 PARLIAMENTARY ELECTIONS (HOUSE OF DEPUTIES)

PARTY[a]	VOTE %	NUMBER OF SEATS	SEAT %
Democratic National Salvation			
Democratic Convention of Romania (CDR)	30.20	122	37.2
Party of Social Democracy in Romania (PDSR)	21.50	91	27.7
Union of Social Democracy (USD)	12.90	53	16.1
Hungarian Democratic Union of			
Romania (UDMR)	6.60	25	7.6
Greater Romania Party (PRM)	4.50	19	5.8
Party of Romanian National Unity (PUNR)	4.40	18	5.6
Total[b]	80.10	328	100.0

Source: Buletin parlamentar, September–December 1996, pp. 4–9.
[a]Includes only those parties and organizations that passed the 3% threshold.
[b]Does not include ethnic-based parties that were awarded a seat per the constitution.

tion government with the USD and the UDMR. The PDSR received approximately 22% of the vote. Since the 1992 parliamentary election, the PDSR had lost about 6% of its electorate while the CDR had increase its share approximately 10%. While the PDSR continued to enjoy popularity among the peasantry, adults over 65 and rural voters, the party did poorly with the country's growing entrepreneurial class, and many working class voters defected from the PDSR to the CDR.[18] The PDSR, and its former coalition partners the PUNR and the PSM, were the clear losers in the parliamentary elections.

In the first round of the presidential election, Iliescu received 32% of the vote while Constantinescu received 28%. Even though Iliescu received a plurality of votes, his first round total was 15% less than in the first round of the 1992 presidential election. Moreover in the first round, several parties including the UDMR and the USD fielded their own presidential candidate, which detracted from Constantinescu's vote share. Although Iliescu received a plurality of the vote, there was concern in the PDSR that he would face a serious challenge in the second round.

With the marginalization of Funar and the PUNR, Iliescu positioned himself as a nationalist. During the two-week period between the first and second rounds of the presidential election, Iliescu's attacks became more vicious and more nationalistic. As the possibility of the UDMR entering the government became more likely, he made a number of anti-Hungarian speeches. He also argued that Constantinescu was a threat to the state and would restore the monarchy. He returned to the familiar theme of the persecution of former communists. Iliescu portrayed himself as a Romanian-style Bill Clinton who could work with the new parliament.[19] This was the first time in Romanian postcommunist politics that a divided government became an electoral issue. There had been speculation that if the CDR formed the new government, then voters in the second round might opt for Iliescu to provide balance. However, the second round of presidential voting indicated that the electorate was not so concerned about divided government as much as competent and honest government. In the second round, Constantinescu received 54.4% of the vote and was elected president.[20] As predicted, he received overwhelming second round support from the UDMR electorate and some support from the USD constituency. Exit polls showed once again that the PDSR had lost the confidence of workers and was less successful in rural areas.

The defeat of Iliescu was an important moment generally in Romanian politics and specifically in Romanian postcommunist politics. This was the first time in sixty years that a head of state was changed by the electorate.[21] Previous heads of state had either died in office or abdicated. Romanian political history has been marred by a lack of respect for the democratic "rules of the game." This election demonstrated a commitment to these rules. Iliescu obeyed the decision of the electorate, followed the constitution and relinquished his office. This was no small feat. Iliescu and the PDSR (in its many incarnations) had dominated the country's politics since 1990. This change in the government says something about Romanian political culture. While a democratic political culture is still evolving, this election and its aftermath showed that no one individual or party was above the democratic process.

FROM OPPOSITION TO GOVERNMENT: THE CIORBEA GOVERNMENT

The CDR received a plurality of the vote and formed a coalition government with the UDMR and the USD. The coalition selected the mayor of Bucharest, Victor Ciorbea, as the new prime minister. Following the success of the CDR, there was a great deal of optimism that necessary economic reforms would finally be enacted by the parliament, and certainly the pace of economic reform was faster under the Ciorbea government than under the Vacariou or the Stolojan governments. In February 1997, the government announced a new program that would reduce government spending, reform the banking system and speed up the privatization of key industries. Based on the reform program, the IMF signed a thirteen-month stand-by agreement in April for US$414 million.

However, during the 1996 national elections, there had been disagreements between the CDR and the USD concerning a pre-electoral agreement. Soon after the formation of the government, Ciorbea and USD leader Roman clashed over the pace of economic reform. Unlike 1990 and 1991, Roman was now advocating a more cautious economic reform program. By the summer of 1997, there was open dissention in the coalition. The pretext for most of the conflict was the issue of economic reform, but in reality much of the conflict stemmed from a clash of personalities. Roman, who was the president of the Senate, indicated in August 1997 that his party would withdraw support from the ruling coalition if the pace of economic reforms continued. The UDMR indicated that it would leave the coalition if the government did not pass an education law that would provide ethnic minorities with linguistic and educational rights.

The Ciorbea government was under constant attack from within the coalition and from opposition parties. In addition, the IMF and the World Bank criticized the government for its lack of progress. In an attempt to placate Roman, Ciorbea reshuffled the cabinet in November 1997. Approximately one-third of the cabinet was changed, particularly in economic-related ministries, and a new Ministry of Privatization was created. The change in these ministries did not ease the tension between Ciorbea and Roman. In December, a USD cabinet member accused the government of being too weak, and Ciorbea demanded an apology. Instead, the member tendered his resignation. This incident provoked Roman to announce that the USD would no longer support the government. To pass the new privatization law, Ciorbea tied the passage of the law to a no-confidence vote. Under parliamentary rules unless a no-confidence vote is offered within three days, the law is considered adopted without debate. To maintain their image as a pro-reformist party, the USD MPs did not table a no-confidence vote. However, this episode finally caused Roman to announce in January 1998 that all four of his party's ministers would withdraw from the government.[22] Although a compromise was worked out, the loss of USD support made passing legislation difficult.

THE VASILE GOVERNMENT

Throughout the spring of 1998, there was an anticipation that the Ciorbea government would resign. The USD provided only tepid parliamentary support to government-sponsored legislation. The CDR-led government needed the support of the USD in parliament to pass its legislative agenda. By March, even members of Ciorbea's own party, the PNTCD, publicly called for his resignation. Finally on 30 March, the entire government resigned and negotiations began immediately over the selection of a new prime minister. The government coalition selected Radu Vasile. Although he was a PNTCD member, his support was primarily from the party's youth wing. The older members, and even Constantinescu, were much less supportive of his nomination. Vasile promised swift economic reform, but few cabinet changes were made. While the 1998 budget was finally passed in the summer, the privatization of key companies such as Romtelecom was delayed.

In January 1999, the same Jiu Valley miners that had descended on Bucharest in 1990 and 1991, began to strike over the closure of several mines. The strike soon turned into a violent march on Bucharest. The marching miners received support from parties such as the PRM and the PDSR. Miron Cozma, leader of the miners' union, had threatened to use force in order to enter Bucharest. President Constantinescu stated that if the violence did not end, he would announce a state of emergency. Finally on 22 January, Prime Minister Vasile met with Cozma to negotiate an agreement. This episode further eroded the public's confidence in the government. The minister of interior resigned and several officers were fired.

CONCLUSION

While the 1996 elections marked an important change in Romanian politics, the promise of economic reform and political stability has not materialized. The current government is a coalition between the CDR, the USD and the UDMR, that are themselves coalitions. The government debates over privatization and education legislation suggest deep divisions between its members. Moreover, the miners' strike in January 1999 demonstrated a lack of confidence in the government and in the political process. Public opinion polls taken in January 1999 showed that only 58% of the public disapproved of the strike. In addition, extremist parties such as the PRM enjoy greater support now than at any other time during the 1990s.

Other East European countries have undergone labor unrest and the development of extremist parties without the violence that has occurred in Romania. The violence of 1999 demonstrates that the country's transition is fragile. The unfinished revolution of 1989 hampers the country's ability to progress. Romania does not possess a civil society in which conflict and disagreement can be resolved through negotiation without the threat of violence. As national elections approach in 2000, the political system has become more divided. Extremist parties enjoy more popular support and the CDR alliance appears disorganized. Given the lack of confidence in the Vasile government, it is possible that Romania will follow an East European pattern of restoring the former ruling party.

The country currently does not possess broad-based parties that can unite the left and the right and bring stability to the political system. Instead, parties are formed around individuals. Over the next few years, there will have to be a consolidation of the party system with the emergence of a few strong parties that no longer rely on personalities. Once these parties enjoy broader support, there will not be a need for party coalitions such as the CDR or the USD. The PNTCD and the PNL will probably emerge as the strongest of the center-right parties while the PDSR and the PD will continue as important center-left parties. Hopefully, the popularity of the extremist parties will decline but that depends on whether the economy will improve. In fact, the consolidation of the party system depends on the ability of politicians to find consensus on economic reform. If the economy remains unstable, then the party system will continue to be fragmented, and nationalist parties will remain a popular alternative to more mainstream parties.

1   Domnita Stefanescu, *Cinci ani din isoria Romaniei* (Bucharest: Editura Masina de scris, 1995), p. 448.

2   *Partidele politice din Romania* (Bucharest: Rompres, 1992), p. 3.

3   Pavel Campeanu, "Opinia publica din Romania in campania electorala," in Pavel Campeanu, Ariadna Combes and Mihnea Berindei, eds., *Romania inainte si dupa 20 Mai* (Bucharest: Humanitas, 1991), p. 29.

4   *Proclamatia de la Timisoara* (Timisoara: The Society Timisoara, 1994), pp. 10–11.

5   Tom Gallagher, "Ultranationalists Take Charge of Transylvania's Capital," *RFE/RL Research Report*, 27 March 1992, p. 23.

6   Campeanu., "Opinia publica din Romania in campania electorala," pp. 58–59.

7   Michael Shafir, "'War of the Roses' in Romania's National Salvation Front," *RFE/RL Research Report*, 24 January 1992, p. 16.

8   Dan Ionescu, "Infighting Shakes Romania's Ruling Party," *RFE/RL Research Report*, 3 April 1992, p. 26.

9   Dan Ionescu, "Romania's Ruling Party Splits after Congress," *RFE/RL Research Report*, 17 April 1992, pp. 8–12.

10 Dan Ionescu, "Another Front for Romania's Salvation," *RFE/RL Research Report* , 21 August, 1992, p. 21.

11 This calculation does not take into account those seats that were awarded to ethnic-based parties as stipulated by the constitution.

12 Michael Shafir, "Romania's Elections: Why the Democratic Convention Lost," *RFE/RL Research Report*, 30 October 1992, p. 7.

13 See for example, Steven D. Roper and William Crowther, "The Institutionalization of the Romanian Parliament: A Case Study of the State-Building Process in Eastern Europe," *Southeastern Political Review*, June 1998, pp. 401–426.

14 Matyas Szabo, "'Historic Reconciliation' Awakens Old Disputes," *Transition*, 8 March 1996, pp. 46–50.

15 Michael Shafir, "Democratic Convention of Romania About to Split?," *OMRI Daily Digest*, 20 February 1995.

16 Ibid.

17 *Romania libera*, 5 June 1996, p. 3.

18 For a complete discussion about the election see, Michael Shafir, "Opting for Political Change," *Transition*, 27 December 1996, pp. 12–17.

19 Iliescu also spoke of the success of French "cohabitation" (the sharing of responsibilities between a prime minister and a president from different parties). In the Fifth Republic, the

French adopted a semi-presidential system in which there was a prime minister and an elected president. Romania is one of the few postcommunist countries that adopted this system.

20 *Libertatae*, 12 November 1996, pp. 1–4.

21 Michael Shafir and Dan Ionescu, "Radical Change in Romania," *Transition*, 7 February 1997, pp. 52–54.

22 "Constitution Watch: Romania," *East European Constitutional Review*, Winter 1998, pp. 27–30.

Chapter 5

One of the factors in the success of the CDR in the November 1996 national elections was the coalition's reformist economic program known as the "Contract with Romania." After six years of slow economic reform, it promised to quickly restructure agriculture and industry, to revitalize privatization and to promote the recovery of the economy. CDR leaders argued that the gradual approach of the PDSR would further undermine the economy and keep Romania behind other East European countries. Following the elections, there was a great deal of optimism regarding the economic program of the Ciorbea government. The population, as well as international organizations such as the IMF, believed that the new government's reform package would significantly speed up the restructuring of the economy. However in-fighting within and between government coalition members stymied attempts at privatization and restructuring. Throughout 1997 and 1998, the country experienced severe economic problems without any real reform. The "shock" without the "therapy" undermined the support for the government and even for President Constantinescu.

As Romania entered the 1990s, the country was in many ways in a better position to pursue economic restructuring than other East European countries. But by the end of the 1990s, any economic advantage that the country possessed has been squandered and reform seems as difficult to implement now as it did in 1990. The CDR-dominated governments held much promise but failed to enact meaningful economic reform. This chapter examines why the Ciorbea and Vasile governments were unable to deliver on their promises of economic reform, and the response of the international community to this failure.

CEAUSESCU'S ECONOMIC LEGACY

As noted in Chapter 3, Ceausescu started an economic austerity program in the 1980s to pay off the country's debt. Most of the US$10 billion that Romania owed was to private Western banks, and rather than rescheduling the debt in installments, he decided to entirely pay it off. To eliminate the debt, Ceausescu started an austerity program in which exports of primary foodstuffs and other domestic agricultural products were dramatically increased while imports substantially declined. For 1988 and 1989, the country repaid a total of US$4 billion of the debt.[1] Romanian economists such as Daniel Daianu and Mugur Isarescu have described Ceausescu's austerity program as a Romanian version of Poland's shock therapy. However, unlike the Polish version, Romanian shock therapy involved import substitution and import switching rather than real economic reform. Moreover, the Romanian version actually increased the level of economic planning and government centralization and concomitantly the level of dissatisfaction and despair among the population.

The irony of the Romanian revolution was that Ceausescu's hated austerity program provided a positive economic legacy to the country in January 1990, unlike any other East European country. By December 1989, Romania had virtually paid off its debt and maintained a current account surplus of US$2.8 billion and foreign exchange reserves of more than US$1.7 billion.[2] In 1989, the country's current account balance, debt-to-GDP ratio and hard currency holdings were better than any other East European country.

DECISIONS MADE AND DECISIONS DELAYED IN 1990

In early 1990, economic advisors to the ruling FSN had a choice between two reform models that were being implemented in other East European countries. The merits and assumptions of the shock therapy or gradual models of economic reform were being debated throughout West and East Europe.[3] In January 1990, Poland adopted the Balcerowicz program that entailed substantial and immediate price liberalization, privatization and stabilization. Unlike Poland, the FSN government decided not to implement shock therapy but instead adopted a gradual approach to economic reform. Mugur Isarescu, Governor of the Bank of Romania, argues that while shock therapy could have been the most beneficial model, it was not feasible for Romania. Firstly, he argues that the shock therapy of the 1980s exhausted the population. It would have been impossible to persuade people to undergo additional sacrifices in 1990 and 1991. Secondly, unlike Hungary and the former Czechoslovakia, which underwent economic reform in the 1980s, the centralization of the Ceausescu austerity program resulted in no institutions, mechanisms or expertise that could immediately assist Romania's production capacity. Finally, Isarescu notes that the collapse of Comecon and the Gulf War significantly reduced the country's foreign trade.[4] Others argue that Romania's initial lack of access to private bank lending increased the cautiousness of the government rather than making it act swiftly.[5]

One of the reasons why the government was so cautious about implementing economic reform was because of its political needs. Between January and May 1990, the FSN provided wage increases (particularly to state workers in inefficient industries), maintained price controls on many goods and promoted an overvalued exchange rate. These actions were taken to increase the party's popularity in preparation for the May 1990 national elections. It was not until the end of 1990 (and after the FSN had secured an overwhelming victory) that the government addressed economic reform. By the time it considered what type of reform program to adopt, the economic gains inherited from the Ceausescu period had disappeared. Romania's US$2.8 billion current account surplus in hard currency became a US$1.6 billion deficit by the end of 1990, and foreign exchange reserves were depleted from US$1.7 billion to less than US$400 million.

The few reforms attempted by the government in 1990 only exacerbated the economic situation. For example, it allowed every worker who had completed a required length of service to retire five years early. This policy was designed to decrease the unemployment that would be associated with economic reform, but the policy had the unforeseen consequence of significantly increasing the demand on the pension system. Within a year of the decision, 400,000 workers had filed for early retirement.[6] Also at the end of 1990, the government finally addressed the issues of price liberalization and the exchange rate regime. In November, the Romanian currency, the leu, was devalued by 60% and prices on some nonessential goods were liberalized.

However, these policies were not accompanied by any state-sponsored privatization. While the government organized state-owned enterprises (SOEs) into commercial companies, no SOEs were actually privatized. Dan Grindea points out that economic reform is only successful if price liberalization and privatization are simultaneously enacted. He argues that price liberalization without privatization encourages hyperinflation.[7] While there was no government-sponsored privatization program in 1990, so-called "spontaneous privatization" occurred in the agricultural sector. In 1990, farm workers dismantled the collective farm system and redistributed land, livestock and materials among themselves.[8] By the end of 1990, a majority of the collective farms had undergone this spontaneous privatization.

THE BEGINNING OF REFORMS IN 1991

By January 1991, the government finally addressed the issue of economic reform. By this time, the country faced a mounting trade and budget deficit, soaring inflation and substantial industrial arrears. Several reasons were earlier noted as to why the government did not impose a shock therapy model of economic reform, but what became clear in 1991 was that an aggressive economic reform package was not supported by a majority of FSN MPs or government ministers. While members of the Roman wing of the FSN favored economic reform, the former *nomenklatura* centered around Iliescu was much more hesitant to implement immediate and often painful reform. As noted in Chapter 4, economic reform was one of the primary issues that led to the break-up of the FSN.

During 1991, the government refused to take any decisive action. The leu became overvalued, and this led to a decrease in exports. While tighter monetary policies were implemented, the monthly inflation average was almost 20%. The loss of export earnings coupled with sagging industrial production contributed to a 13% decrease in GDP. The loss of industrial production was both an economic and political issue for the government. During 1991, industries amassed arrears amongst themselves in order to finance their operations. By the end of 1991, these interenterprise arrears amounted to 50% of GDP.[9] These arrears contributed to hyperinflation, a loss of economic productivity and had a political consequence. The protests by the Jiu Valley miners in September 1991 that caused the "resignation" of the Roman government were instigated because of inflation and salary concerns. The parliament eventually passed a law that provided for an expansion of bank credit to clear all interenterprise arrears.

EFFORTS AT PRIVATIZATION

The deteriorating economic situation forced Romania to sign a stand-by agreement with the IMF in 1991. Part of the performance criteria specified in the agreement called for a devaluation of the leu and privatization of the industrial sector. The parliament passed a law that codified the spontaneous agricultural privatization. The land ownership law ended the practice of collective farms and returned land to over seven million people. However, families received parcels of land that were less than ten hectares. The law never clearly defined the concept of property rights,[10] and few individuals actually received titles to their property.[11] Also, by limiting the distribution of land to ten hectares, the government created too many small and commercially inefficient farms. However, from a political perspective, the government had given land to a large number of potential voters.

While the process of agricultural privatization was inefficient, it was carried out rather quickly. Industrial privatization was much more economically and politically difficult to implement. During 1990 and 1991 approximately 6,300 SOEs were turned into joint-stock commercial companies with 70% of their capital distributed to the State Ownership Fund (SOF) and the remaining 30% distributed to one of five Private Ownership Funds (POFs) that were formally owned by the population. The remaining SOEs were turned into what are called *regies autonomes* (RAs). These RAs remained under state ownership and reported directly to the Ministry of Finance. They possessed quasi-commercial and state functions and were normally either natural monopolies, utilities or companies identified as important to national security. Approximately 450 SOEs were transformed into RAs, including some of the largest and most important industries such as the Romanian electric monopoly Renel.

The parliament passed the privatization law in August 1991 that became the basis of the first mass privatization program (MPP). All of the commercial companies registered in 1990 and 1991 were subject to privatization. The law provided numerous ways in which SOEs could be privatized including open auctions and tenders, initial public offerings (IPOs) and management-employee buyouts (MEBOs). The law also required the free distribution of fifteen million certificates of ownership to all adults. These certificates were part of the 30% of capital owned by the POFs. They could be freely traded among individuals, converted into shares of a company owned by a POF, retained as an ownership interest in a POF or converted at a later date into shares of investment fund companies created from the dismantling of the POFs. The law envisioned that 70% of capital owned by the SOF would be privatized for cash; however for large and medium size commercial companies, the SOF relied mostly on direct sales to investors.

The first phase of the MPP encountered several organizational problems and political resistance even in the government. Firstly, the certificates were issued to the population before the SOF and the POFs were established.[12] For a period of time, individuals could not dispose of their certificates and companies could not be privatized. Secondly, even when the POFs were established, they were reluctant to exchange

shares in their best companies for the certificates though the population formally owned the POFs. Part of the problem was that while the
law stipulated that the population owned the POFs, the law also
designated the POFs as the issuers of ownership certificates and
allowed them to determine the process for share exchange.[13] To cover
the losses of other companies, the SOF rarely sold the best companies
in its portfolio. Companies that represented politically powerful con-
stituencies were not privatized and continued running deficits. All of
these factors contributed to lower levels of foreign direct investment
than in almost any other East European country.

EXPORT-LED GROWTH?

By 1992, the Stolojan government recognized that the economic situation required a reorientation in macroeconomic policy. The government cautiously pursued a combined strategy of further price
liberalization, wage stabilization and austerity (to combat inflation)
with export concessions (to boost capital inflows).[14] The idea was that
greater export earnings and increases in direct foreign investment
would offset the economic problems associated with a currency
devaluation and higher interest rates. Therefore in early 1992, the leu
was devalued, interest rates were raised to 80%, export licensing was
terminated, and there was a reduction in the number of goods that
were subject to export quotas. The government wanted to eliminate
the currency black market by devaluing the leu. There was a fear that
this would lead to an increase in inflation, but policy-makers determined that improving the country's trade deficit and stimulating
growth was more important.

These policies were pursued in order to increase the level of domestic output. By 1992, output had fallen 25% from 1989 levels.[15] One of
the reasons for this decline was the further deterioration of Romania's
industrial sector. Because of the failure to significantly privatize this
sector and provide necessary capital, output further declined. While
export concessions were granted to these industries, they did not
produce products that could be exported. The other problem with
industrial development was that these industries were highly inefficient
in their use of energy. This export-led growth policy created a vicious
circle because in order to export goods, industries needed increasing
amounts of energy imports that the government subsidized. Although
the government continued to subsidize energy imports, industrial
unemployment increased by over 12%.[16] Unemployment in branches

such as textiles and machine building was especially high. The "labor shedding" in industry was necessary to raise levels of productivity, but other sectors were not much more profitable. Because of structural reasons and a terrible drought in 1992, Romania continued as a net food importer. However, the *private* agricultural sector was highly productive. To increase agricultural efficiency and output, the government needed to privatize the intermediate stages of agricultural production.

This export-led growth policy was adopted not only to increase domestic output but also to redirect patterns of trade. Because of the disintegration of Comecon and the Soviet Union, the country increased its trade relations with OECD countries. Among all East European countries during this period, Romania and Slovenia achieved the greatest redirection of trade flows away from Comecon countries towards OECD countries, particularly EU member-states.[17] The problem with this pattern of trade, however, was that while overall trade increased, EU imports almost doubled in 1992.[18]

Early economic gains in 1992 were erased by the end of the year. While inflation declined in early 1992, the yearly inflation rate was still almost 200% (see Table 5.1). The trade deficit did not improve and GDP decreased almost 9% from 1991 levels. The export-led growth policy was unsuccessful because political needs prevented real economic reform. Daniel Daianu, minister of finance, argues that the September national elections prevented the government from really pursuing an export-led model of development.[19] The market-oriented exchange rate regime adopted earlier in the year was terminated, and the government re-established control over the rate. In July, the parliament passed several amendments to the law governing unemployment benefits that provided additional benefits with an indexation of wages.[20] Between October and December 1992, the black market

TABLE 5.1   SELECTED ECONOMIC INDICATORS: 1991–1997

INDICATOR	1991	1992	1993	1994	1995	1996	1997
Real GDP (Percentage Growth)	−12.9	−8.7	1.5	3.9	7.1	4.1	−6.6
Unemployment Rate (Percentage)	2.4	7.4	9.5	9.5	7.4	6.1	7.4
Inflation (Average Percentage)	222.8	199.2	295.5	61.7	27.8	56.9	45.0
Current Account Balance (Billions US$)	−1.3	−1.5	−1.2	−0.5	−1.7	−2.3	−2.4
Gross External Debt (Billions US$)	2.1	3.3	4.3	5.5	6.8	9.1	9.3

Sources: "Romania–Recent Economic Developments," *IMF Staff Country Report*, No. 97/46, (Washington, D.C.: International Monetary Fund, 1997), p. 64. *Buletin Lunar*, 4/53, (Bucharest: National Bank of Romania, 1998), pp. 15–17.

reappeared as the leu became overvalued. As a consequence of this exchange policy, exports declined and the trade deficit increased. In addition, the global compensation policy enacted in 1991 and 1992 to eliminate interenterprise arrears failed to prevent a new accumulation of arrears. This was important because these arrears provided an extra source of liquidity to the market, and therefore higher interest rates could not lower inflation.

EU ASSOCIATE MEMBERSHIP

Although the end of 1992 did not provide a basis for optimism regarding the economy, several positive events occurred in 1993 that helped to stabilize the situation. With the elections concluded, the Vacariou government finally addressed economic reform. One of the important developments in that year was the association agreement that Romania signed with the EU on 1 February 1993. In June 1993 the EU European Council acknowledged that the goal of these East European association agreements was to assist the countries in attaining full membership. Although the performance of the Romanian economy in 1992 was far below that of the Czech Republic, Hungary or Poland, the EU had signed association agreements with countries that had had economies similar to Romania in the 1980s. The economies of Greece, Spain and Portugal were also in a period of transition when they gained full EU membership in the 1980s.[21]

The EU granted the country associate status because it increased the amount of trade. Romania was the second largest East European market. Between 1993 and 1995, trade between Romania and the EU almost doubled. Since 1992, the EU has benefited from a trade surplus with the country.[22] Aside from the economic considerations, there were important political and foreign policy reasons why the EU signed this agreement.

Like Greece, Spain and Portugal during the EU second enlargement, political criteria were deemed more important for associate membership than economic criteria. The EU European Council in June 1993 established political criteria for full membership: stability of democratic institutions, the rule of law, human rights and protection of minorities. In Romania, membership of organizations such as the EU was viewed as a vehicle to promote the consolidation of democracy. Both the EU and the Council of Europe played a significant role in the development of legislation regarding human and minority rights. Also in the area of foreign policy, the Romanian government portrayed itself as a pole of stability in the Balkans. The problems in the former Yugoslavia and concerns about signing an agreement with Hungary and not Romania were foreign policy issues that Brussels considered. While Romania's association agreement was an important first step in the process of EU integration, it was the first step in a process that will take decades.[23] Ultimately, the association agreement was signed because the economic costs to the EU were low and the political and foreign policy benefits were more substantial.

PRIVATIZATION BEGINS

While the legal framework for the MPP was established in 1991, very little privatization occurred in 1992 (only twenty-two SOEs were privatized).[24] The lack of privatization was attributed to organizational problems, a lack of information on companies and an inability to attract foreign direct investment. By 1993, some of these problems were solved and over 260 companies were privatized. While the overall number of privatized companies increased, 92% of the companies privatized in 1993 were small SOEs, and almost all of them were privatized through the use of MEBOs in which employees were able to exchange their certificates for their 30% share held by the POFs.[25] The privatization of large enterprises was much slower. For example, out of 708 large SOEs included on the 1990 privatization list, only two were privatized by 1993. Part of the difficulty in privatizing these large SOEs involved the economic and ultimately political issue of industrial unemployment. Because most SOEs were privatized through the use of MEBOs and were small enterprises, privatization contributed only a small increase in unemployment. Although unemployment increased in 1992, the level of unemployment stabilized in 1993 and rose only about 2%. While 1993 marked the real beginning of the MPP, the reluctance to privatize large SOEs and restructure the industrial sector had economic and political consequences for Romania for the rest of the decade.

Although the government in 1993 lacked the political will to sustain economic restructuring, it imposed several policies designed to contain monetary growth. These policies were necessary because the country experienced a period of hyperinflation in 1993. The annual inflation rate was almost 300%, and the monthly inflation rate peaked in May at almost 31%. As a consequence, the government imposed fiscal and monetary austerity measures to provide monetary stability. Firstly, the government cut subsidies and reduced spending on goods and services.

This decreased the budget deficit from 4.6% of GDP to less than 1%, but it also increased the level of poverty, which approached 20% by the end of 1993.[26] Secondly, the Vacariou government consolidated the tax system and introduced a value-added tax (VAT). Thirdly, there were further efforts at trade liberalization that increased the amount of exports and reduced the trade deficit. Fourthly the government benefited from continuing assistance from official creditors. During the period between 1990 and 1994, financing from official creditors, including the IMF and the World Bank, averaged over US$1 billion annually.[27]

The net result of these policies was that GDP registered its first positive gain since 1990 (see Table 5.1). Not only did GDP increase by 1.5% compared to 1992, but the industrial sector, which benefited from the easing of export restrictions and the EU association agreement, posted its first positive contribution to GDP in three years.[28] The Vacariou government argued that these achievements indicated a new phase in the country's transition; however, GDP was still 26% less than the 1989 level, and the industrial contribution to GDP was almost 45% less than 1989 figures.

Without a pending election, the government continued many of these reforms in 1994. The government continued to liberalize prices, control public spending and stabilize the currency. As a consequence of these fiscal and monetary policies, annual inflation dropped from 300% to 61% in 1994 (see Table 5.1). Exports were strong, and the annual trade deficit decreased from a high of US$1.4 billion in 1992 to US$500 million in 1994. The trade deficit with the EU went from US$816 million in 1993 to US$266 million in 1994.[29] By 1994, the EU was Romania's primary commercial partner. This policy of export-led growth increased domestic output, and 1994 GDP registered a positive 3.9%. Because of the measures that the government undertook, the IMF signed another stand-by agreement in April 1994.

A HOUSE OF CARDS

In 1995, the Vacariou government continued promoting exports and reducing social spending. Exports increased by US$1.8 billion, annual inflation was less than 28% and GDP was 6.9%. However, these figures masked serious problems in the economy. While exports grew, import demand increased substantially, and the economy recorded its highest annual trade deficit of US$1.6 billion in 1995.[30] While the inflation rate dropped, the budget deficit and external debt increased. Although the government instituted several measures designed to stabilize the economy, there were three fundamental problems with the government's strategy. Firstly, the government's fiscal and monetary restraint was characterized by a stop-and-go policy. Measures were introduced to limit wage increases and within six months rescinded. The leu was devalued and then the National Bank provided emergency credits to state sectors. The fundamental problem in the government was that no one was willing to consistently apply economic reform policies. Measures were implemented and as soon as an important political constituency complained, for example miners or steel workers, the measures were lifted. Because the PDSR's political strength came from state workers, it failed to provide the political leadership necessary for economic reforms. Moreover, many PDSR members were not convinced that IMF-sponsored economic reforms were correct, and they were very reluctant to support the privatization of large SOEs. When the party formed an open coalition government with several extremist parties, the repudiation of the Western economic model became even more public.

Secondly, the reductions in public spending subsidies were targeted primarily at the Social Fund (i.e., unemployment and pension benefits). While the prices of certain goods were liberalized between 1993–1995, many important goods, particularly energy, were still heavily subsidized by the government. These subsidies contributed to a mounting budget deficit. In addition, the government subsidized the industrial sector. By 1995, industrial interenterprise arrears again developed, and wages in the sector were more than double productivity.

Thirdly, the government never seriously addressed the issue of economic restructuring. The government instituted fiscal and monetary reforms, but never dealt with the issue of privatization and industrial reorganization. By 1995, less than 25% of commercial companies identified in 1990 were privatized and only 8% of large SOEs were privatized.[31] There developed a dichotomy in the industrial and agricultural sectors. While Romania achieved impressive export growth, most of this growth came from the private sector not industrial SOEs or state agricultural farms. GDP growth was limited because most of the economy was still in the hands of the state. The government realized that to sustain economic growth it had to restructure the failed privatization program.

The lack of privatization between 1993–1995 forced the government to pass a new mass privatization law. The program started in mid-1995, and new free vouchers were issued to every adult who had not used their previous certificates.[32] Unlike the certificates, these new vouchers could not be transferred or sold. They could only be exchanged for shares in the 3,900 companies that were offered. Only 30% of the shares of any company were offered as part of the second MPP, with the remaining shares belonging to the SOF. The offered shares were set at a fixed price and could not be negotiated. Individuals could either exchange their vouchers for shares or entrust their vouchers to a POF.

The distribution of the vouchers was completed by September 1995, and 31 December was established as the deadline for exchanging these vouchers. Because of a lack of information and education regarding the new program, only 26% of the vouchers were exchanged by the deadline.[33] It was repeatedly extended until 1 May 1996 by which time when 93% of the vouchers had been exchanged. More than 80% of the SOEs offered were privatized through the use of MEBOs. The problem with this method was that it did not provide an infusion of capital necessary to modernize an industry. After May 1996, many of these companies were still not fully privatized, and none of the import-ant RAs such as Renel or Romtelecom, were part of the second MPP. If the goal of mass privatization was to place shares in the hands of the population, then the second MPP was a success. Most of the popu-lation now had shares in commercial companies. But, if the goal of mass privatization was to foster an entrepreneurial spirit among the population, then the second MPP was a failure. Individuals invested their vouchers with little or no information about the company, and the enterprises that were privatized had a poor capital base. One public opinion poll taken in November 1995 found that 36% of respondents did not understand the process and 70% could not iden-tify the institutions in charge of privatization.[34] The failures of the MPP became part of the political debate surrounding the 1996 national elections.

The economic reforms and partial successes of 1994 had vanished by the time of the 1996 national elections. Economic conditions deterio-rated throughout 1996. While GDP remained positive, the budget and trade deficit grew. In 1996, the country's current account balance (as a percentage of GDP) increased to 6.6%, and the external debt increased by almost a third. The inability to control wage increases, especially in an election year, led to a 30% increase in annual inflation in 1996.[35] Unlike the period between 1991–1994 when Romania received substantial financing from international lenders, official creditors only lent approximately US$50 million during 1995–1996.[36] Because of the failure to address energy subsidization and industrial privatization, the IMF in 1995 delayed the release of tranches negotiated in the 1994 stand-by agreement.

By 1996, the country's hard currency reserves were severely depleted, and when the government could not import more energy to offset the terrible weather conditions, several factories closed sending workers onto the streets.[37] Throughout 1996, the government tried to keep prices low for energy and basic foodstuffs, but two devaluations of the leu forced the government to increase prices. All these factors contributed to low levels of foreign direct investment. In 1996, foreign direct investment had declined by almost 50% to just US$210 million.[38]

During the election campaign, the CDR's "Contract" focused on turning family farms into more viable commercial enterprises (consolidating the small plots allowed under the law), promoting industrial restructuring and instituting transparency in the privatization process. Presidential candidate Constantinescu promised to resign if some of the urgent economic reforms were not enacted. As discussed in Chapter 4, the PDSR had no new campaign ideas and focused on the same scare tactics that had worked in 1992. It argued that a CDR government would expropriate land and seek retribution against communist party members. There was no clear message about what the PDSR would do to stop the economy's free fall. The CDR's program specifically stated the measures that its government would support to stabilize the economy and restore domestic and international confidence in the country.

THE CIORBEA GOVERNMENT

The victory of the opposition created a great deal of optimism on the part of the population and Western leaders that the country would finally seriously address the economy's structural problems and implement the painful but necessary reforms that the CDR had promised. However, the new government was in fact a coalition within a coalition. The CDR members included the PNTCD, the PNL and other single issue or right-of-center parties. The CDR formed the government coalition with the USD and the UDMR. While there was general agreement during the election on the need for economic reform, the implementation of policy was stymied by the personality conflicts between these parties. In a national address, Prime Minister Ciorbea accused the Vacariou government of concealing the real extent of the country's economic problems, and he stated that the budget deficit was actually three times higher than the reported figure.

In December 1996, the Ciorbea government presented to parliament a new economic program that included a reduction in energy subsidies for industry and residents and a lifting of price supports for most basic commodities and public transportation. Shortly after the program was announced, domestic crude oil prices increased and placed inflationary pressures on the economy. The inflation rate during the first quarter of 1997 was 76.5%, and tariffs for urban transportation increased by 121%. In early 1997, the government further lifted price supports on basic staples, and the prices for items such as bread increased by almost 155%[39] The government packaged together a number of economic reforms into an omnibus bill that the parliament could vote up or down but could not amend. As a consequence, the government passed reforms on unemployment benefits, land restitution and placed the SOF under the control of the government rather than the parliament. The government also quickly passed a new budget that reduced industrial and agricultural subsidies.

Because of the actions that the government undertook, the IMF signed a new thirteen-month stand-by agreement in April 1997. It agreed to a US$414 million package designed to assist in the restructuring of the economy. The government agreed to liberalize the exchange rate regime, eliminate direct credits from the National Bank to industries and the agriculture sector (in order to reduce overall market liquidity) and reduce the external current account deficit from 6.6% of GDP in 1996 to 4.5% of GDP in 1997.

By mid-1997, the government was finally starting economic reforms that were necessary to make the economy more competitive and modern, but soon after three problems arose that ultimately prevented it from implementing the reforms. Firstly, there was a great deal of dissension among coalition members. The PNTCD strongly backed a measure to return nationalized property to individuals, but the USD, and especially the PD, opposed the plan. The PD and its leader Roman were closely linked to business interests that wanted to stymie efforts at economic reform in order to prevent competition and maintain generous government subsidies. The acrimony between Ciorbea and Roman continued throughout the year and created a crisis in the coalition.

Secondly, the Ciorbea cabinet discovered that it was extremely difficult to purge PDSR loyalists from the government ministries. Though Ciorbea replaced the heads of the SOF and the Ministry of Privatization, many middle management and staff members were not replaced. These individuals were much less supportive of the government's economic reforms. Also, state banks continued the practice of providing emergency credits to inefficient industries. Because there was no privatization in the banking sector, these state banks held a great deal of economic and political influence. The problem for the new government was that it was attempting to radically change an administrative structure that had developed over a period of years. There were entrenched interests that would lose economic and political power if restructuring occurred.

Thirdly, the government sometimes created its own problems by taking actions designed to reform the economy without properly preparing the population. While polls conducted immediately before and after the elections found that the population was generally supportive of economic reform, the government failed to provide the proper education necessary to make individuals supportive of specific measures. For example, the government's initial list of SOEs to be closed was quickly announced without any significant publicity. When officials attempted to enter the enterprises, workers protested and rioted. Eventually, several of these enterprises were taken off the list. In order to placate workers that would be laid-off when their factory closed, the government announced a generous severance package. Soon afterwards, workers in various sectors began to voluntarily quit. By September, approximately 84,000 had received severance benefits worth US$140 million, and as a consequence by the end of 1997 one of the problems with the Social Fund was the high ratio of recipients to contributing workers.[40] Because of the underground economy, only half of all workers contributed to the Social Fund.[41]

By September 1997, it was clear that the ambitious economic reform program was running into problems. Several SOEs were either taken off the closure list or the privatization process was handled so poorly that bidding was canceled. For example, the privatization of Romania's largest petrochemical factory, Petromidia, was postponed because two of the bidding companies had not filed the necessary forms with the SOF. While the World Bank and United States Agency for International Development issued a report recommending four possible methods for the restructuring of Renel (state electric company) as early as February 1996, by 1998 the SOF still had not developed a comprehensive plan to restructure the energy sector.[42] During 1997, the head of the SOF, Sorin Dimitru, became a focal point of criticism. Many blamed the slow pace of privatization on him. Unlike Ciorbea, who wanted speedy privatization, Dimitru wanted privatization based on a "quality criterion" in which fewer SOEs would be privatized but for a larger sum of money. Dimitru asserted his own privatization schedule because of the support from President Constantinescu. Although Constantinescu had no constitutional authority to maintain Dimitru in his position, Ciorbea and the cabinet deferred to him on this matter.

DETERIORATING MACROECONOMIC AND POLITICAL CONDITIONS

Like Vacariou, Ciorbea was unable to sustain economic reform. While the government lifted price supports, it also provided severance pay to workers. The government placed many SOEs on the closure list, and then never actually closed the enterprises. The inability to follow a consistent course of action caused friction in the coalition and led to a loss of popular support for economic reform. The problem was that the population was experiencing all of the shock but none of the therapy of reform. While the government decreased the trade deficit, the external debt service ratio expanded to 25% of exports. Servicing the debt was a significant drain on the budget. By the end of 1997, the inflation rate reached a four-year high of 151% while GDP shrank by almost 7% (see Table 5.1). While SOEs distributed large wage and salary benefits, industrial output declined even further from 1996 levels.[43]

Given the state of the economy, the EU Commission in its July 1997 Agenda 2000 Report indicated that while Romania had made some economic progress since the 1996 national elections, Romanian businesses were not ready to compete with EU counterparts. The Commission recommended that the country not be included in the first round of negotiations, and at the December 1997 Luxembourg Summit, the EU European Council agreed with the Commission's recommendation. While this decision was hardly surprising, it followed on the heels of the Madrid decision on NATO enlargement (which also did not include Romania). In both cases, the government and population placed a great deal of importance on integration into these Euro-Atlantic institutions. The government was in the difficult position of defending its economic polices without having tangible successes, either at home or abroad.

The lack of economic restructuring was caused by and contributed to friction among the coalition members. Roman and the USD were particularly critical of Ciorbea and his economic policies. Although Roman portrayed himself as an advocate of speedy reform, he was slowing the pace of privatization. The coalition disagreements and lack of a consistent policy caused the IMF's delegation head to accuse the government of violating several parts of the stand-by agreement. At the end of 1997, the IMF refused to release tranches that were part of the April stand-by agreement. However for many of the nationalist parties, the IMF and the World Bank were the causes of the country's problems.

As discussed in Chapter 4, the criticisms within and outside the government forced Ciorbea to reshuffle the cabinet in November 1997. A total of seven ministerial positions were changed, including finance, reform and privatization. The new individuals appointed to these ministries were considered to be nonpartisan professionals. The change in these ministries, however, did not alleviate the antagonism between Ciorbea and Roman. The irony was that the hyperinflation of 1997 had been significantly reduced by 1998. For the first quarter, the monthly inflation rate was 4.6% (compared to 17.2% during the same period in 1997).[44] While Ciorbea could point to some moderate economic successes in early 1998, the issues that divided these men were political, and in January all USD ministers withdrew from the cabinet.[45] Finally in March 1998, Ciorbea resigned as prime minister, and Vasile was nominated.

THE VASILE GOVERNMENT

The Vasile cabinet presented to parliament in April 1998 was very similar to the previous cabinet, but one change was that Dimitru was appointed minister of privatization. Dimitru combined this position with his position as head of the SOF. Rather than being demoted because of the failures of the SOF, he was actually given even greater responsibility over the privatization process. Dimitru's supporters argued that the problems in the privatization program occurred because of institutional conflict and red tape. With Dimitru head of both the Ministry of Privatization and the SOF, his supporters claimed that the privatization process would be much smoother.

The reaction of the international community to the new government was cautious. The IMF was much more reserved in its support. In April, an IMF delegation met with the new government and indicated that negotiations would only begin when the 1998 budget was passed. At these meetings, the government announced that it was privatizing some of the RAs and other state holdings, as required by the IMF. By May, the last stand-by agreement expired with more than US$220 million unused. Also in May, the parliament finally passed the 1998 budget which projected an annual inflation rate of 45%, a budget deficit of 3.5% and a 4% decrease of GDP. However, the government missed the 31 May deadline for the restructuring of Renel and postponed the sale of Romtelecom from July to September.

The problem for the Vasile government was that Roman and other members of the USD had little interest in promoting economic reform. The conflict over reform and personality that typified the Ciorbea government did not end. What had changed was the level of public dissatisfaction. The inability to restructure the economy and to improve the economic situation had a negative impact on the popularity of the CDR and Constantinescu, and as a consequence, the government, the president and the coalition were pointing fingers. In October, Dimitru resigned as head of the SOF and minister of privatization. The public criticisms of him caused Constantinescu to withdraw his support. In November 1998, Finance Minister Daniel Daianu was dismissed because of his failure to reform the ministry; although, he was widely perceived as one of the few reformers in the cabinet. Also in November, the EU Commission issued its annual accession report that was very critical of the government's macroeconomic policies. The head of the EU delegation for Romania stated that "the reform process has slowed down; the state could not impose financial discipline in the sector of public enterprises and did not attack difficulties in the financial sector."[46]

CONCLUSION

As Romania began the decade of the 1990s, it was in one of the best fiscal and monetary positions of any East European country. The country had no external debt and substantial foreign exchange reserves. The problem was that no one in the FSN leadership was ready to capitalize on these advantages and introduce the necessary and painful economic reforms. Instead, the budget and trade deficit increased, privatization was practically nonexistent and corruption in government ministries was rampant. Within a year, Romania squandered its economic advantage and adopted a stop-and-start process of economic reform that ultimately devastated the economy. While the official statistics portrayed a reforming economy by the mid-1990s, there was no doubt that the country was considerably behind other East European countries. Perhaps given the level of economic reform that had occurred in these countries prior to 1989 and the level of centralization in Romania under Ceausescu, it was not surprising that the Visegrad economies of the Czech Republic, Hungary and Poland were much healthier. The question is whether the Roman, the Stolojan and the Vacariou governments could have implemented reforms to stop Romania's free fall. While the Stolojan and Vacariou governments attempted some reforms, they were piecemeal and never consistently applied.

The 1996 elections and the formation of the new coalition government was supposed to mark the real beginning of economic reforms, but the Ciorbea and the Vasile governments were ineffective in restructuring the economy. While there was a recognition on the part of these governments that economic restructuring had to occur, in-fighting among coalition members prevented the implementation of promised reforms. The people have suffered terribly since 1996, and international organizations are now more skeptical of the commitment and promises of the government. As a Romanian commentator explained "the credibility so easily lost by the Ciorbea Government is going to be extremely hard to recover by the Vasile Cabinet."[47]

The credibility of the Vasile government was itself severely shaken during the miners' march to Bucharest in January 1999. The miners were protesting the closure of several mines and factories and demanding an increase in wages. Initially the Vasile government refused to negotiate with the miners, but after several outbreaks of violence, Prime Minister Vasile finally met with miners' union leader Cozma. Although the text of the agreement was never made public, Cozma stated that the government agreed to a 10% wage increase, revoked the closure of two mines and would provide US$200 million to the Jiu Valley area to cover the cost of reform. The government, however, denied that the wage increases would be paid by the state (instead the factories would pay the increases). The government also stated that the closure of the two mines was only postponed, not revoked.

Ultimately, the differences in the interpretation of this agreement could lead to renewed calls by miners to strike or march on Bucharest. In addition, any government increases in worker wages would make discussions with the IMF more difficult.

As discussed in Chapter 3, the social costs of Ceausescu's austerity program were one of the precipitating factors of the revolution. After almost a decade of food lines, shortages of fuel and heating in homes, schools and factories, the people demanded an economic change. Compared with almost all other Eastern European societies in the 1980s, Romanian society was the most economically deprived. When compared to other East European countries today, Romania ranks at or near the bottom in several economic categories, and the country continues to lag well behind the Visegrad economies.

The economic situation would improve if a consensus could be reached on economic reform. Previous governments have recognized the necessity of reform but failed to implement long lasting measures. The major economic goal of the country is full membership in the EU. But in order to join the EU, Romania over the next decade will have to carry out painful reforms that politicians and large segments of the population have resisted. If the country fails to implement these reforms, it will fall even further behind its East European neighbors.

1 Daniel Daianu, "Dilemmas of the Stabilization Policy in Romania," *Sfera politicii*, April 1993, pp. 12–13.

2 Ibid.

3 For a general discussion of these models and the choices made by various East European countries see, Bernard Chavance, *The Transformation of Communist Systems: Economic Reform Since the 1950s* (Boulder, CO: Westview Press, 1994); Andras Koves and Paul Marer, eds., *Foreign Economic Liberalization: Transformations in Socialist and Market Economies* (Boulder, CO: Westview Press, 1991); Peter Havlik, ed., *Dismantling the Command Economy in Eastern Europe* (Boulder, CO: Westview Press, 1991).

4 Mugur Isarescu, "Monetary Policy, Macroeconomic Stabilization and Banking Reform in Romania 1995," *Central European Issues*, Winter 1995/1996, pp. 25–40.

5 Daniel Daianu, "Dilemmas of the Stabilization Policy in Romania," p. 13.

6 "Romania—Recent Economic Developments and Selected Background Studies," *IMF Staff Country Report*, No. 96/9, (Washington, D.C.: International Monetary Fund, 1996), p. 33.

7 Dan Grindea, *Shock Therapy and Privatization: An Analysis of Romania's Economic Reform* (New York: Columbia University Press, 1997), p. 39.

8 "Romania—Recent Economic Developments," *IMF Staff Country Report*, No. 97/46, (Washington, D.C.: International Monetary Fund, 1997), p. 64.

9 Mugur Constantin Isarescu, "Monetary Policy and Inter-Enterprise Arrears in Romania," *Sfera politicii*, December 1992, p. 20.

10 Dan Grindea, *Shock Therapy and Privatization: An Analysis of Romania's Economic Reform*, pp. 82–83.

11   John S. Earle, "Unemployment Policies in Romania (II)," *Sfera politicii*, February 1994, pp. 24–25.

12   "Romania—Recent Economic Developments," *IMF Staff Country Report*, p. 24.

13   Dan Grindea, *Shock Therapy and Privatization: An Analysis of Romania's Economic Reform*, p. 66.

14   Daniel Daianu, "Dilemmas of the Stabilization Policy in Romania," p. 13.

15   Alexandru Radocea, "Economic Revival—Prerequisite of Romania's Integration into European Structures," *Romanian Journal of International Affairs*, December 1996, p. 60.

16   John S. Earle, "Unemployment Policies in Romania," *Sfera politicii*, January 1994, pp. 14–15.

17   Ben Slay, "External Transformation in the Post-Communist Economies: Overview and Progress," in Michael Kraus and Ronald D. Liebowitz, eds., *Russia & Eastern Europe After Communism: The Search for New Political, Economic, and Security Systems* (Boulder, CO: Westview Press, 1996), pp. 65–89.

18   Mihai Berinde, "The European Agreement—An Important Stage in the Development of Mutual Trade Relations," *Romanian Journal of International Affairs*, December 1996, pp. 164–172.

19   Daniel Daianu, "Dilemmas of the Stabilization Policy in Romania," p. 13.

20   John S. Earle, "Unemployment Policies in Romania (II)," p. 24

21   Steven D. Roper, "The European Community as an Agent of Reform: EC Admission Criteria and Romania," *The American Review of Politics*, Spring 1994, pp. 105–121.

22   Mihai Berinde, "The European Agreement—An Important Stage in the Development of Mutual Trade Relations," pp. 167–168.

23   For example, Turkey has had an association agreement with the EU since the 1960s.

24   "Romania—Recent Economic Developments and Selected Background Studies-Statistical Appendix," *IMF Staff Country Report*, No. 96/10, (Washington, D.C.: International Monetary Fund, 1996), p. 23.

25   A small enterprise was defined as an enterprise with capital of less than 2.5 billion lei or about US$33 million in 1991 dollars and less than 500 employees.

26   "Romania—Recent Economic Developments," *IMF Staff Country Report*, p. 32.

27   Ibid, p. 51.

28   Alexandru Radocea, "Economic Revival—Prerequisite of Romania's Integration into European Structures," p. 61.

29   Mihai Berinde, "The European Agreement—An Important Stage in the Development of Mutual Trade Relations," p. 167.

30   "Romania—Recent Economic Developments," p. 5.

31   "Romania—Recent Economic Developments and Selected Background Studies-Statistical Appendix," p. 23.

32   Those individuals that had not used their certificates were allowed to invest them, but they retained their original face value of 25,000 lei (about US$12 in mid-1995). Each voucher had a face value of 975,000 lei (approximately US$425 when issued in mid-1995).

33   "Romania—Recent Economic Developments," p. 25.

34   Lavinia Stan, "Romanian Privatization Program: Catching Up with the East," in Lavinia Stan, ed., *Romania in Transition* (Aldershot: Dartmouth Publishing, 1997), p. 154.

35   *Raportul anual 1996* (Bucharest: Banca Nationala a Romaniei, 1997).

36   "Romania—Recent Economic Developments," p. 51.

37   Michael Shafir and Dan Ionescu, "Radical Political Change in Romania," *Transition*, 7 February 1997, pp. 52–54.

38   "Romania—Recent Economic Developments," p. 55.

39   *Quarterly Bulletin 1/1997* (Bucharest: National Bank of Romania, 1997).

40   "Constitution Watch: Romania," *East European Constitutional Review*, Fall 1997, pp. 32–35.

41   Mihail Galatanu and Adriana Halpert, "Romania este paradisul muncii la negru," *Capital*, 20 November 1997, p. 1.

42   Mircea Caster and Petre Barbu, "Monopolul electricitatii isi pierde energia," *Capital*, 27 February 1997, p. 11.

43 *Quarterly Bulletin 4/1997* (Bucharest: National Bank of Romania, 1997).

44 *Monthly Statistical Bulletin 4/1998* (Bucharest: National Commission for Statistics, 1998).

45 "Constitution Watch: Romania," *East European Constitutional Review*, Winter 1998, pp. 27–30.

46 Livia Saplacan, "European Commission Criticizes Romania's Economic Performance," *Romania Libera*, 9 November 1998, p. 8.

47 Liana Simion, "Do We Still Have the Green Light?," *Invest Romania*, Summer 1998, p. 35.

Chapter 6

During the 1980s, Romanian foreign policy underwent a dramatic change. As noted in Chapter 3, the country in the late 1960s and throughout the 1970s had the most Western-oriented foreign policy of any Warsaw Pact member. Presidents Nixon and Ford visited the country, and it was one of the first Eastern European countries to join organizations such as the IMF and the GATT. Romania developed good trade relations with Western Europe and received American MFN status. Ceausescu served as a mediator in several international conflicts in Africa and in Asia. The country's foreign policy was described as "maverick" and "autonomous" from the Soviet Union. However by the mid-1980s, Ceausescu's regime turned increasingly paranoid and anti-Western. Romanian treatment of ethnic Hungarians and religious groups became a major concern to countries such as the United States. To pay off its foreign debt, the country turned increasingly towards the Soviet Union for trade and energy needs.

As a consequence of Ceausescu's policies, Romania emerged after December 1989 much more isolated than almost any other East European country. Several countries including Poland, Hungary and even Bulgaria started their "return to Europe" well before Romania.[1] Moreover, the perceived lack of democracy, economic reform and the poor treatment of ethnic minorities in the early 1990s also hindered the country's foreign policy. Domestic politics inhibited the country's foreign policy goal of European integration. The 1996 elections marked a change in domestic and foreign policy initiatives. Romanians hoped that the newly elected government would hasten the process of integration into Euro-Atlantic structures such as the EU and NATO. While the member-states of the EU and NATO noted the progress that the country had made under the Ciorbea government, Romania could not catch up with the Visegrad countries and was not included in the first wave of EU or NATO accession talks. These had been the two foreign policy priorities of the Ciorbea government.

In order to understand these foreign policy issues, this chapter examines how the internationalization of ethnic issues and lack of economic reform hampered the country's foreign policy. The status of ethnic minorities, particularly ethnic Hungarians, was a major impediment to its foreign policy goals, and the lack of economic reform made EU accession negotiations problematic. This chapter explores Romania's four primary foreign policy concerns: integration into the EU and NATO and relations with Hungary and the Republic of Moldova.

THE NEW EUROPEAN ENVIRONMENT

While a return to Europe was a goal of the FSN since its inception, domestic events, sometimes instigated by the government itself, stymied the country's efforts to become a member of Euro-Atlantic organizations. Confrontations between ethnic Romanians and ethnic Hungarians in the city of Targu Mures in March 1990 and the use of miners by President Iliescu to suppress opposition in June called into question Romania's adherence to democratic values. By the end of 1990, the West perceived the FSN as a neo-communist organization. Unlike Solidarity or Charter '77, the FSN lacked democratic credentials and the vast majority of its members were the former *nomenklatura*. The West therefore maintained pressure on the FSN for greater political and economic reform.

Romanians were also divided over the definition of European integration. For the ruling FSN, integration was an institutionally-driven process. Integration was associated with membership in institutions such as the EU and the Council of Europe. For the opposition, integration was a domestic, social process. The country needed to become more democratic, to reform the economy, to tolerate ethnic diversity and to allow the expression of opposition in the media.[2] In other words, the opposition believed that the country needed to integrate the society before the country could integrate into Europe. These competing views of integration influenced Romanian foreign policy throughout the 1990s. The FSN successor governments focused most of their attention on the institutional issues of integration without fully appreciating the need to make substantial domestic reforms. No issue hampered their foreign policy objectives more than the status of the country's ethnic Hungarians.

THE DEBATE BETWEEN HUNGARY AND ROMANIA

The treatment of ethnic Hungarians was always a central issue in Romanian-Hungarian bilateral relations, but the American debate over Romania's MFN status in the 1980s demonstrated that the status of ethnic minorities was a broader foreign policy issue. Immediately following the revolution, there was a great deal of goodwill between ethnic groups. However as discussed in Chapter 4, clashes in Targu Mures in March 1990 between ethnic Hungarians and Romanians left several dead and hundreds injured. The event galvanized both ethnic Romanian and Hungarian extremists. The Hungarian government viewed the violence as a continuation of Ceausescu's policy of forced ethnic assimilation.

While the FSN officially abandoned Ceausescu's policy that minority relations were an internal matter, Iliescu and Prime Minister Roman defended their minority policy against attacks from "outside inter-ference" (i.e., the Hungarian government). The rhetoric coming from Budapest often confirmed the worst fears of Romanians. The Hungarian government spoke of the special relationship between the "motherland" and the Hungarian nation.[3] While Hungary was not claiming international jurisdiction over Hungarians living abroad, the government maintained that it was obliged to ensure the observance of Hungarian human rights. The Romanian government stated that it viewed such a principle as domestic interference.

The Hungarian government insisted that measures needed to be taken to secure the rights of Romania's ethnic Hungarians. The Hungarian government identified several concrete steps that would demonstrate goodwill on the part of the Romanian government. Firstly, the Hungarian government advocated the opening of a consulate in the Transylvanian city of Cluj to serve the large ethnic Hungarian commu-nity in the city. Secondly, it urged the creation of a Hungarian-language university to replace the previous one in Cluj that was forcibly merged with another university in 1959. Thirdly, the Hungarian government sought the creation of cultural centers that would ensure that Hungarian-language books and educational material would be available.

For the Hungarian government, these steps provided a basis for the creation of collective or group rights for Romania's ethnic Hungarians. While ethnic Hungarians enjoyed individual rights, and even some col-lective rights such as the guarantee of a seat in the lower house of par-liament, Budapest felt that the individuals' rights enshrined in the Romanian constitution did not sufficiently protect minorities.[4] It insisted that the Romanian government ensure the collective rights of ethnic Hungarians. The Romanian government argued that collective rights had no legal basis and that the extension of such rights violated several sections of the constitution.

While the Hungarian government was concerned with the issue of collective rights, the Romanian government was principally concerned with ensuring its territorial integrity, namely the Transylvanian border with Hungary. Romania insisted that its relationship with Hungary should be based on a clear recognition of the current boarders between the two states. Hungarian Prime Minister Jozsef Antall argued, however, that the request was unnecessary because international conventions already ensured European borders. In essence, both sides viewed the request of the other as unnecessary and provocative. In order for the two countries to enjoy good relations and sign a basic treaty of friendship, it would be necessary for these issues to be resolved.

THE ROLE OF ROMANIAN ETHNIC HUNGARIANS

The status of Romania's ethnic Hungarians continues to be a primary issue for several leading Hungarian and Romanian parties. In Romania, ethnic Hungarian parties and cultural organizations banded together in December 1989 to form the UDMR. Tokes, one of the symbols of the revolution, was named honorary president. According to the platform of the UDMR, one of its goals is to integrate the country's ethnic Hungarians into "universal Hungarian cultural circles."[5]

The UDMR is a coalition of several ethnic Hungarian parties and cultural organizations. It claims over 500,000 members and has been one of the members of the post-1996 CDR-led coalition governments. The UDMR has been concerned with a broad range of issues including the right of local self-government, right of expression, education in the mother tongue and regional autonomy. At its Third Congress in 1993, the UDMR adopted a declaration that stated that the ethnic Hungarian community possessed the right to self-determination, which it claimed did not violate Romania's territorial integrity. Because the UDMR is a coalition, there exist within the organization various interpretations and definitions of concepts such as self-determination and regional autonomy. For UDMR radicals, autonomy means the creation of a local ethnic Hungarian parliament with veto power over national legislation. Other groups have adopted a much more moderate view of autonomy and self-administration.[6] The UDMR played an active role in negotiations between Hungary and Romania. The Hungarian government routinely consulted with the UDMR leadership and the party held discussions with officials from institutions such as the Council of Europe and the EU. The UDMR insisted that it be included in any negotiation over the status of

Romania's ethnic Hungarians. Because of this active domestic and international role, the UDMR came under intense criticism from nationalist parties such as the PUNR and the PRM. Funar, the former chair of the PUNR, is mayor of Cluj. He called for the UDMR to be outlawed and imposed local ordinances designed to limit Hungarian cultural expression. While his tactics were extreme, he represents a segment of the population that does not trust the UDMR agenda. Tudor, president of the PRM, also attacked the UDMR as a Budapest surrogate in Romania. Both the PUNR and the PRM called on the government to end any discussions with Hungary. Nationalist parties and policies were not limited to Romania. Hungarian nationalists also urged their government to break off talks with Romania.[7]

ETHNICITY AND INTEGRATION

The status of Romania's ethnic Hungarians and the dispute between Hungary and Romania was more internationalized after 1990. Negotiations between these two countries became part of their larger international agenda. Organizations such as NATO and the EU were clear to both parties that signing a basic treaty and resolving the status of ethnic Hungarians was critical to their admission into these and other Euro-Atlantic structures. To secure admission into the "New Europe," the international community placed pressure on both sides to find a compromise.

The Romanian search for Euro-Atlantic integration was a search for a new definition of Europe. Many Romanians questioned in which part of Europe their country belonged. The foreign policy establishment considered the country's association with the Balkans to be detrimental to its integration into Europe. They believed that the West was more concerned about the economic and military security of Central Europe. Teodor Melescanu, foreign minister during the 1990s, argued that Romania is a Central European state. He stated that excluding some Central European states such as Romania from Euro-Atlantic integration would disturb the "geopolitical balance of Central Europe."[8] Other Romanians are less clear about which geographic zone Romania belongs to.[9]

The country's foreign policy was predicated on two other concerns. Firstly, there was the concern over whether integration was a coherent, all-inclusive process or differentiated. In other words, whether it was possible for Romania to be included in European economic integration but not European military integration. The government's position was that integration should not proceed on an issue-by-issue basis but rather that there should be a comprehensive approach.[10] Military, economic and political integration should proceed in unison. Perhaps one of the reasons why the government maintained this position was because it wanted to use its membership in other European institutions such as the Council of Europe as a basis for membership in additional organizations such as NATO or the EU.

Secondly, the government insisted that while good relations with Central European states was a foreign policy priority, the status of Romania's ethnic Hungarians was a purely domestic issue. For much of the 1990s, the government resisted attempts to internationalize the status of ethnic Hungarians by both the Hungarian government and the UDMR. Some Romanian politicians maintained that the discussion on minority rights was a pretext for territorial revision. In a speech on human rights, Iliescu argued that there are "governments and political forces who tend to use the very noble preoccupation with the protection of minority rights as a substitute for putting forward territorial claims, which otherwise can in no way be accepted by the international community."[11] While the government dismissed the status of ethnic Hungarians as a foreign policy issue, European institutions insisted that the protection of minority rights was a fundamental condition of membership.

THE COUNCIL OF EUROPE

One of the first European institutions that Romania started membership discussions with was the Council of Europe. While not an important economic or military organization, membership in the Council of Europe was considered important because it would demonstrate that Romania was part of Europe. In early 1990, a Council of Europe fact-finding mission visited Romania to discuss its impending application. Within days of this visit, the country tendered its application.[12] However, it was derailed by the events in Targu Mures in 1990 and the violent episode involving the Jiu Valley miners in September 1991. While Hungary was admitted to the Council of Europe in 1990, followed by Poland in 1991 and Bulgaria in 1992, Romania only held guest status. During 1992 and 1993, Council of Europe commission reporters Friedrich Konig and Gunnar Jansson made repeated trips to Bucharest to investigate human rights issues and the status of ethnic Hungarians. During the discussions, UDMR members urged the Council of Europe not to approve the country's application. In addition, the Hungarian government protested Romania's human rights record.

After much debate, the Council of Europe's Committee of Ministers voted in 1993 to ratify the admission of Romania (Hungary abstained from the vote). The Committee of Ministers noted, however, that the country's progress on minority rights would be closely monitored and that this was the beginning of a process and not an end. In March and April of 1994, another delegation headed by Konig and Jansson collected information regarding the progress on minority rights. Tokes, the UDMR's honorary president, took this opportunity to denounce the government's compliance with the recommendations of the Council of Europe. The UDMR and Hungary accused the Romanian government of not following the obligations of Council of Europe membership. After 1996, the situation between the Council of Europe and Romania improved. The Council decided that monitoring the country was no longer required.

THE EU

Although membership in the Council of Europe was regarded as important, the EU was viewed as the most important European institution. Adrian Nastase stated that "when talking about the European integration, one generally refers to the accession to the European Union."[13] As discussed in Chapter 5, the first round of negotiations for Romania's association agreement started in May 1992. The EU accession criteria are based on the political, economic and foreign policies of applicant states. An applicant state must demonstrate a democratic political system that respects fundamental human and political rights. The Romanian government insisted that the 1990 and the 1992 national elections demonstrated a commitment to democratic elections. Similar to countries such as Greece and Spain during the EU's second enlargement, Romania maintained that membership in the EU would provide a foundation for the strengthening of democracy in the country.[14]

The EU is concerned not only with the policy objectives of applicant states but also the perception of the EU among the citizens of applicant countries. During the second enlargement, domestic political support was essential to gaining membership.[15] Surveys conducted in 1995 showed overwhelming Romanian popular support for EU membership. When asked whether they would vote for EU membership in a referendum, 97% of Romanians surveyed responded "yes," the highest figure in East Europe.[16]

On 1 February 1993, Romania signed an association agreement with the EU that eliminated 90% of all quotas and tariffs imposed on industrial imports. Dan Ionescu argues that the association agreement was an indication of the country's acceptance of "the same moral and political values as those of Western Europe, especially with respect to human rights in general and the rights of minorities in particular."[17] On 1 February 1995, the association agreement came into force. In June 1993, the European Council in Copenhagen stated that these agreements with Central European states were a preparatory stage towards full EU membership. At a European Council meeting in Essen in December 1994, the EU decided that discussions on full membership would be extended to all associate members, and on 22 June 1995, Romania submitted its formal application for EU membership.[18]

To demonstrate the broad support for its application, all parliamentary parties convened at a conference on 21 June 1995 (the day before the formal application was submitted) and signed a statement agreeing to a common integration strategy.[19] Since then however, several parties including the PRM and the PUNR have raised concerns over the process of European integration. Joined by the Romanian Orthodox Church, these parties have denounced the passage of several EU-inspired laws, for instance the legalization of homosexuality.

Although nationalist parties were much less supportive of EU membership, the Ciorbea and Vasile governments made integration into Euro-Atlantic structures a foreign policy priority. Based on the principles announced at Essen, Romania pursued EU membership. In the "Agenda 2000" communication issued in July 1997, the EU Commission indicated that while the country had made substantial political progress since the 1996 national elections, Romanian businesses were not ready to compete with EU counterparts. The EU Commission recommended that the country not be included in the first round of integration. Constantin Ene, the Romanian ambassador to the EU, noted that the Commission's opinion would have a great deal of influence in the EU Council's decision-making process.[20] Indeed at the December 1997 Luxembourg Summit, the EU Council agreed with the Commission's recommendation. In November 1998, the Commission issued a report on Romania's progress towards accession. In this report, the Commission listed several reasons why the country was not named a "fast-track" applicant. The report noted that Romania's political situation and foreign policy was generally aligned with the EU but that economic conditions were disturbing. The report cited several economic problems, including limited privatization, only a small amount of foreign direct investment and a lack of financial discipline.

The reaction in Bucharest to these reports was divided. The government and President Constantinescu acknowledged that the economy had not attracted significant foreign investment or undergone substantial reform. The government pledged to work with the EU on these economic issues to ensure the country's speedy integration. However the nationalists and their supporters denounced the report as proof that the West would never accept the country into European institutions. Even after finding a compromise with Hungary, Romania's position in East Europe had not changed. The PRM and the PUNR used the situation to condemn the basic treaty that the country had signed with Hungary.

THE HUNGARIAN BASIC TREATY

As noted earlier, the West demanded that a basic treaty be signed with Hungary before Romania would be considered a serious candidate for NATO or EU membership. Integration into Euro-Atlantic structures internationalized the basic treaty with Hungary and placed pressure on the Vacariou government and Iliescu to find a compromise. During 1994 and into 1995, Romanian and Hungarian negotiators attempted to formulate a treaty. One of the major obstacles to the negotiations was the Council of Europe's Recommendation 1201. This document expanded ethnic minority rights in the area of local public administrative procedures, and the Hungarian government insisted that it be included in the basic treaty. What was of particular concern was Article 11 of Recommendation 1201, which stated that in areas where they are a majority, ethnic minorities should have "at their disposal appropriate local or autonomous authorities or ... have a special status matching the specific historical and territorial situation."

The Vacariou government opposed linking Romania's bilateral relationship with Hungary to the larger issue of Euro-Atlantic integration. Moreover, the government maintained that such a linkage damaged the discussions with Hungary. The concern was that the lack of a basic treaty would be used as a justification for a partial enlargement in which Hungary and not Romania would be included. Melescanu stated that a partial enlargement of NATO "does not help at all the current and complex process of the Romanian-Hungarian negotiations on a political treaty. Instead of settling a problem, such an approach would create other more complex problems."[21]

While the Vacariou government denied the linkage between the basic treaty and Euro-Atlantic integration, there was little doubt in 1995 and 1996 that Euro-Atlantic integration was a major issue that brought the two parties together. In March 1995, the two negotiating teams announced that their discussions had failed because of the insistence of the Hungarian team to include a reference in the treaty to Recommendation 1201. While Vacariou and Iliescu realized the necessity of finalizing a basic treaty with Hungary, domestic concerns were more important. As discussed in Chapter 4, in January 1995 the PDSR signed a protocol with the PRM, the PUNR and the PSM. These parties agreed to support the PDSR in exchange for a coordination of legislation, particularly on ethnic issues. Therefore even if the PDSR had wanted in 1995 to include in the basic treaty the language of Recommendation 1201, the need to maintain the coalition government proved more important.

Not only were the nationalist parties opposed to the language contained in Recommendation 1201, several opposition parties including the PNTCD spoke out against the Recommendation.[22] Other CDR members were opposed to the Recommendation being included in the basic treaty for fear that it would provide a basis for ethnic Hungarian claims of territorial autonomy. The opposition's position was complicated by the fact that the UDMR was affiliated with the CDR. This division became even more important when these parties formed the government coalition in 1996.

Throughout 1995, the negotiations remained at an impasse. Finally in August, Iliescu made a surprise announcement of a new proposal for reconciliation between the two countries.[23] Iliescu's proposal included the drafting of three documents: a joint declaration on the reconciliation, a "code of conduct" on the treatment of ethnic minorities and a basic treaty (Recommendation 1201 was not mentioned in the proposal). The reaction to Iliescu's proposal was divided. In the West, the proposal was well-received as an attempt to jump-start the negotiations that had failed in 1994. The Hungarian government was more reserved and stated that any basic treaty would have to be premised on the protection of minority interests. Most of the criticism over the proposal came from within Romania and particularly from members of the government coalition. The PRM stated that Iliescu's announcement was a capitulation to the UDMR and the Hungarian government. Because of its position on this issue, the PRM was shortly removed from the coalition.

Throughout 1996, pressure to sign a treaty on both Hungary and Romania increased. During 1996, NATO and EU officials held discussions in Budapest and Bucharest concerning enlargement. Both organizations stressed that accession was for those countries that would not present a security dilemma. While the position of these organizations was the same, a couple of factors combined to give the negotiations impetus. Firstly, the Hungarian government under Prime Minister Gyula Horn was more receptive than the previous Antall government to negotiations. Secondly, with national elections scheduled in late 1996, Iliescu and the PDSR leadership wanted to elevate the country's standing abroad and at home. While Iliescu knew that an agreement with Hungary would not be popular with some segments of society, he also knew that the lack of an agreement was a fundamental obstacle towards Romanian Euro-Atlantic integration.

After several bilateral negotiations, a final compromise was reached in August 1996. The Hungarian government agreed to a clause that confirmed the "inviolability of their common border and the territorial integrity of the other Party" while the Romanian government agreed to include a paragraph enforcing those rights that were provided for in Recommendation 1201. However, the Romanian government negotiated a clause that stated that the Recommendation "does not refer to collective rights, nor does it obligate Parties to grant those persons the right to a special territorial autonomy status based on ethnic criteria." This compromise satisfied the Hungarian government because the Recommendation was included in the text, while the Romanian government was content because Hungary recognized its territorial integrity and ensured that the Recommendation would not be interpreted as a guarantee of collective rights for ethnic Hungarians. While the two governments were satisfied with this compromise, both Romanian nationalists and the UDMR denounced it. The PUNR leadership objected to the inclusion of Recommendation 1201 and declared it an act of treason. As a consequence, the PUNR was removed from the coalition. The UDMR leadership also stated the compromise was an act of betrayal.[24]

Both prime ministers in Timisoara signed the basic treaty on 15 September 1996, and after a quick review by the Romanian parliament, the treaty came into force on 8 October. The Hungarian parliament ratified the treaty on 10 December. The Romanian government wanted to finalize the treaty before the November national elections. The irony was that during these elections, Iliescu positioned himself as a nationalist. Iliescu argued that a CDR-UDMR government would enact a federal system of government and dismantle the state. While Iliescu and the PDSR had resolved one of the obstacles to Euro-Atlantic integration, the electorate was not convinced that Iliescu or a PDSR government would enact the economic and political reforms necessary for further integration. The victory of the CDR sent a signal to the EU and NATO that the country was willing to address reform.

NATO MEMBERSHIP

While EU membership was viewed as the major long-term foreign policy priority, NATO membership was considered the most important short-term objective of the Ciorbea government and President Constantinescu. This emphasis on NATO membership was actually a continuation of the Vacariou government. Melescanu stated that "while the adjustment to EU standards would imply a reasonable period of transition, security needs are immediate and can become stringent."[25] To address its security needs, Romania was the first country to sign the Partnership for Peace (PfP) program in January 1994. The PfP is a NATO initiative designed to encourage practical collaboration between NATO and PfP members. The PfP Framework Document lists several areas of cooperation, including the "facilitation of transparency in national defense planning and budgeting processes; ensuring democratic control of defense forces; the development of cooperative military relations with NATO … [and] the development, over the longer term, of forces that are better able to operate with those of the members of the North Atlantic Alliance."

Although not specifically stated in the Framework Document, the government believed that the PfP program was a transition stage to NATO membership, and therefore the country was very active in the PfP program. In 1995, Romania hosted two major PfP exercises and participated in six PfP activities abroad.[26] By 1996, the country had participated in 960 activities with NATO member forces. Between 1994 and 1996, Romania signed thirty-one bilateral military agreements.[27] While political relations with Hungary were tense, military cooperation was excellent. In fact, Romania had almost twice as many military activities with Hungary than with any other East European country.

While EU membership entailed significant economic reforms that were politically difficult, NATO membership required military modernization and interoperability that was much easier to finance and attain.[28] In a speech to the North Atlantic Council in 1997, President Constantinescu stated that "Romania will be capable to bear the cost of her integration into NATO."[29] After the national elections in November 1996, there was a renewed effort to ensure that the country was part of the first wave of NATO expansion. The government pointed to several factors in its favor. Firstly, it was claimed that the peaceful change of government in November indicated that the country was fully committed to democratic principles. Secondly, the ratification of the basic treaty with Hungary had resolved the issue of NATO importing a security dilemma. Thirdly, the participation of the UDMR in the coalition government was further proof of the country's commitment to minority rights. Fourthly, Romania was continuing its active participation and support of the PfP program, and fifthly, the government argued that admission was critical to NATO, given the country's geographic location.

During 1997, the Ciorbea government mounted a publicity campaign designed to rally support for NATO membership. The media coverage devoted to this issue was enormous. Pro-TV, the highly popular independent television station, ran a contest in which Romanians sent in pro-NATO postcards for entry in a drawing of prizes. Surveys conducted found that public support for NATO admission was the highest of any East European country. Surveys found that while only 59% of the Hungarian public favored NATO membership, 95% of the Romanian public supported membership.[30]

The government maintained that only NATO membership could provide the country with a true measure of security. While the military continued to participate in the PfP program, the government stated that it did not view the PfP as a security substitute for NATO. Constantin Ene, the liaison ambassador to NATO, stated that selective enlargement would create security and strategic concerns that participation in the PfP would not alleviate.[31] The United States took a different view. Secretary of Defense William Perry stated that "many Partner nations are starting to see PfP as important in and of itself, irrespective of NATO membership."[32] Perhaps other nations viewed the PfP program as an end, but the Romanian government always viewed it as a means to the end of NATO membership.

As in the case of EU enlargement, NATO expansion became a domestic political issue for member-states. Countries such as France and, to a lesser extent, Germany and Italy voiced early support for Romania's admission. France and Romania always enjoyed close relations, but other countries such as the United States were much more reserved in the assessment. Finally in June 1997, the United States announced that it would only support the candidacies of the Czech Republic, Hungary and Poland. The Clinton administration believed that while the Ciorbea government had made significant reforms, Romania needed more time to transform its economy and allow democracy to mature. At the Madrid Summit on 8 July 1997, NATO heads of state concurred with the American position and did not invite the country to begin accession discussions. While Slovenia and Romania received considerable attention, NATO European member-states agreed with the American position.

Although the United States did not support Romania's application in the first wave, the Clinton administration maintained an open-door admission policy. To prove this point, President Clinton traveled to Bucharest shortly after the conclusion of the Madrid Summit. There he stated that he believed that the country would become a member of NATO, but he felt that the country needed more time before it could accept the "burden" of membership. In Romania, the decision of the United States and NATO was seen by some as "another Yalta." Prime Minister Ciorbea and President Constantinescu had devoted much of their time to this issue and while the government maintained that the Madrid decision had only increased its resolve to join NATO, many in the press viewed the decision as a major setback for the CDR.[33] Since July 1997, the government has been much more realistic about the possibility of NATO membership. Prime Minister Vasile noted that while NATO membership was a major foreign policy priority, he did not expect it before 2003. Moreover he explained that in future discussions over NATO membership, he wanted to avoid "the hysteria" that accompanied the 1997 bid.[34]

REPUBLIC OF MOLDOVA

While Romanian foreign policy in the 1990s focused on the rights of indigenous ethnic groups, another major focus of the country's foreign policy was the status of ethnic Moldovans in the former Soviet Republic of Moldova. In Moldova, there are approximately 2.8 million ethnic Moldovans, and they constitute the country's largest ethnic population group (64.5%). For Romanians, Moldova is considered part of the historic lands of the state and nation, and ethnic Moldovans are ethnic Romanians. The Moldavian Prince Stephen the Great is honored in Romania as a national hero. The Moldavian principality united with Wallachia in 1859 to form modern Romania, and the territory of present-day Moldova roughly corresponds to the area of historic Bessarabia that was incorporated into Greater Romania following World War II.[35] This area was relinquished to the Soviet Union in 1940 as part of Molotov-Ribbentrop Pact. The Romanian army reclaimed the area in 1941, and Moldova only became a Soviet Republic in 1944.[36] From the 1940s until the early 1990s, the Soviet Union permitted very limited contact between Romania and Moldova. Throughout this period, the Soviet leadership encouraged the creation of a distinct Moldovan nation. As part of the Russification policy, the alphabet for the Romanian language changed from Latin to Cyrillic, and Russian became the language of interethnic communication, higher education and public life.

In 1987, Moldovan intellectuals, as part of Gorbachev's policy of *glasnost*, organized informal discussion groups that focused on issues of language and culture.[37] Within a year, these informal groups had organized formally around the issue of linguistic and cultural freedom. By 1989, the pro-Romanian and pro-unionist movement, Popular Front (*Frontul Popular* or FP), became the leading Moldovan opposition force. The FP received tacit support from many communists, and several leading FP members were actually ranking communist party members. Moldova's last Soviet-era parliament was elected in March 1990. The composition of the parliamentary and government leadership reflected the FP dominance. The parliament chose Mircea Snegur as president of Moldova (he was popularly elected president in 1991). During this period, the FP pursued a pro-Romanian and even pro-unionist agenda that alienated the Russian minority. In August 1990 the Gagauzi, a Turkic Christian minority located in Southern Moldova, announced the formation of their own republic followed shortly in September by the same announcement from authorities in Transnistria, a region situated on the left bank of the Dniester River. The Romanian government expressed its concern over the increasing hostilities in Moldova.

ROMANIAN VIEWS ON MOLDOVA

From 1944 to 1964, Romanian historians accepted the official Soviet view that Moldova was "reunited" not united with Russia, based on the acceptance of a "proposal" from the Soviet Union.[38] The

Romanian view of Moldova during this period was always tempered by the need to placate the Soviet leadership. However as noted in Chapter 3, the 1964 "declaration of independence" signaled a change in the Romanian attitude towards the Soviet Union and even towards the "Bessarabian issue." In 1964, Romanian historians were allowed to re-examine the Soviet occupation of Moldova, and Ceausescu in 1965 and 1966 continued Gheorghiu-Dej's policy of supporting historians who were critical of the Soviet official position.[39] They never directly attacked the Soviet position, but throughout the Ceausescu period, historians argued that Moldova was a Romanian territory.

After December 1989, the situation in both Romania and Moldova substantially changed. Romania started the process of democratization, and Moldova asserted its right to determine its own linguistic policies. Cultural and educational contacts between the two countries were quickly re-established after 1989, and the Romanian government urged Gorbachev to open the Moldovan border. After Moldova proclaimed its independence on 27 August 1991, the Romanian government adopted a two-track policy. On the one hand, Romania was the first country to recognize Moldova's independence; on the other hand, Romanian political leaders articulated a policy of eventually reunification. Adrian Nastase, the foreign minister at the time, stated that the reunification of Romania and Moldova would occur based on the German model, but he never offered a precise date.

The 1992 Moldovan civil war with Transnistria occurred during the Romanian pre-electoral campaign and received a great deal of attention from candidates and parties. The Transnistrian forces received manpower and materials from the Russian 14th Army stationed in the Transnistrian capital of Tiraspol. As the war of words turned into a full-scale civil war, Romania played an increasing role as diplomatic supporter of Moldova.[40] While Romanian politicians maintained the position that Moldova was an independent state and that reunification was the decision of the Moldovan people, President Iliescu stated that Romanian recognition of Moldovan independence did not imply a "renunciation of the rights" that had been taken by the Molotov-Ribbentrop Pact.[41]

Although the "Moldovan card" was an attempt by Romanian politicians to mobilize voters, it was not very successful. While political leaders viewed Moldova as an important domestic and foreign policy issue, the electorate was much less interested and much less enthusiastic about reunification. In May 1992, only 17% of

Romanians desired reunification with Moldova, and only 4% favored military assistance during the civil war.[42] Given the lack of public support it is not surprising that reunification has not become an important foreign policy issue. While the CDR, and specifically the PNTCD, was a leading force in the call for reunification, it was never a top foreign policy priority of the government. Moreover, the economic problems in both countries make the application of a German model of reunification very improbable. Neither country is economically prepared to bear the costs of reunification.

MOLDOVAN VIEWS ON REUNIFICATION

The Romanian government maintained that reunification was a Moldovan decision. In 1991 and 1992, Moldovan President Snegur maintained a policy of "one people, two states." Throughout 1991 and 1992, Snegur resisted calls for reunification and the pro-Romanian FP lost much of its parliamentary and public support in 1992 and 1993, culminating in a stinging defeat in the 1994 parliamentary elections with the party receiving less than 10% of the vote. The Moldovan public's zeal for reunification had clearly waned, and in 1994 a "popular consultation" was held on the question of statehood. An overwhelming 95% of the electorate voted for the continuation of Moldovan statehood.[43] This result was not surprising considering that even in 1992, less than 15% of ethnic Moldovans had favored reunification.[44] By this time, President Snegur had changed his position and articulated a policy of a Moldovan "multiethnic" state. Although in 1996 Snegur attempted to change the constitution and rename the state language Romanian, he maintained a pro-independence position. During the 1996 presidential election Snegur and his chief opponent, Petru Lucinschi, both articulated a pro-independence position.

ROMANIAN-MOLDOVAN RELATIONS SINCE 1996

After Lucinschi's victory in 1996, contacts between the two countries increased. Presidents Constantinescu and Lucinschi met on several occasions to discuss regional security and economic development. While there was greater cultural and economic cooperation, the two countries have not signed a basic treaty. Part of the problem involves a Romanian demand for a specific reference to the Molotov-Ribbentrop Pact. Several Romanian intellectuals criticized the country's foreign policy for being too obsessed with the Pact.[45] Although Moldova continued to be an issue, Romanian foreign policy was much more oriented towards the West than the East. It is unclear what impact Romanian integration into Euro-Atlantic structures would have on the possibility of reunification with Moldova. On the one hand, Romanian EU membership would provide Moldova an economic incentive for reunification because of access to the EU market. But Romanian membership in NATO would further delay the possibility of reunification. NATO membership has much less support in Moldova, and in fact, the country has taken a neutral military position.

ROMANIAN RELATIONS WITH UKRAINE

The other country that figures prominently in any discussion of Greater Romania is Ukraine. The area of Northern Bukovina that was once part of Greater Romania is now in Ukraine. While a great deal of international attention has focused on the treatment Romanian ethnic minorities, little attention has been paid to the treatment of the ethnic Romanian minority in other countries. An interesting case involves the approximately 135,000 ethnic Romanians in Ukraine. In the area of Northern Bukovina, ethnic Romanians constitute 20% of the population.[46] Much like their ethnic Hungarian counterparts in Romania, ethnic Romanians in Ukraine asserted their right to cultural autonomy. The General Congress of Romanians of North Bukovina demanded the creation of a free border zone in the Cernauti region, and during Ukrainian elections in April 1994, the Romanian press was highly critical of the electoral law governing minority candidates.[47] Most of the Ukrainian parties were portrayed as unsympathetic to the demands of the ethnic Romanian minority.

The status of ethnic Romanians frustrated the negotiations over a basic treaty. The Romanian government wanted the treaty to include a reunification of the Molotov-Ribbentrop Pact, which gave Romanian lands to Ukraine, and a reference to Recommendation 1201. While the Romanian government hesitated on including the Recommendation in its treaty with Hungary, it demanded that reference to the Recommendation be included in the Ukrainian treaty. These two demands prevented any agreement, but as in the Hungarian case, NATO membership prompted the Romanian government to seek a comprise. In 1997, Ukraine and Romania signed a basic treaty that did not refer to the Pact, but did contain the Recommendation and recognized the territorial integrity of both countries. President Constantinescu and President Leonid Kuchma of Ukraine have met on several occasions to discuss greater economic and regional cooperation.

CONCLUSION

The election of Constantinescu and the creation of a CDR-led government coalition gave many Romanians the hope that the country finally would be recognized as a European rather than a Balkan country. The PDSR government's commitment to democracy was questioned in Western circles, and finally in 1996 the electorate chose a new leadership to implement democratic and market reform. While Euro-Atlantic institutions recognized the political and democratic progress that Romania made, the lack of economic reform became a roadblock to EU membership. Now EU and NATO membership are considered long-term goals, and nationalist parties and ideologues are denouncing the NATO and the EU-inspired treaties that the country signed with Hungary and Ukraine. As Romanian foreign policy enters the 21st century, domestic economic reform will largely dictate the pace of Euro-Atlantic integration. While the country is now firmly established in Europe, it must wait behind several other countries in the queue for European integration.

The revolution ended a process of Romanian isolation from the West. While the country began the 1980s with close relations with the West, these relations became strained during the decade. Ceausescu unilaterally ended MFN with the United States, and several European governments and the United States spoke out against Ceausescu's ethnic minority and religious policies. While the revolution ended this isolation, it did not end criticisms of the country's ethnic, political and economic policies. Part of the unfinished revolution is the quest for full integration into the new Europe and Euro-Atlantic organizations. While Romania has made some progress (e.g., membership of the Council of Europe and associate member status in the EU), the integration of the country into Europe will take years if not decades.

1   For example, Bulgaria, Hungary and Poland received guest status from the Council of Europe in 1989.
2   Vladimir Socor, "Foreign Policy in 1990," *RFE: Report on Eastern Europe*, 28 December 1990, pp. 28–29.
3   Edith Oltay, "Minority Rights Still an Issue in Hungarian-Romanian Relations," *RFE/RL Research Report*, 20 March 1992, p. 16.
4   The Romanian constitution in Section 2 of Article 59 guarantees organizations that represent national minorities one seat in the lower house only if the organization fails to garner an outright seat. Both in 1992 and 1996, the UDMR received over 7% of the vote and an average of twenty-six seats in the House of Deputies.

5   Crisan Iliescu and Cristina Roman, "Sintezele platformelor electorale ale partidelor care au obtinut peste 1% din voturi," in Petre Datculescu and Klaus Liepelt, eds., *Renaterea unei democratii alegerile din Romania de la 20 mai 1990* (Bucharest: IRSOP, 1991), pp. 178–180.

6   Michael Shafir, "The Congress of the Hungarian Democratic Federation of Romania: Postponed Confrontations," *Sfera politicii*, February 1993, pp. 11–12.

7   Matyas Szabo, "'Historic Reconciliation' Awakens Old Disputes," *Transition*, 8 March 1996, pp. 46–50.

8   Teodor Melescanu, "The National Security of Romania: Priorities and Legitimate Concerns," *Central European Issues*, Autumn 1995, pp. 16–31.

9   Eugen Preda, "Vecinii vecinilor nostri sunt ca si vecinii nostri," *Sfera politicii*, November 1993, pp. 24–25.

10 Teodor Melescanu, "The National Security of Romania: Priorities and Legitimate Concerns," p. 26.

11 Ion Iliescu, *Romania in Europe and in the World* (Bucharest: Romania Publishers, 1994), p. 79.

12 Liviu Ion, "Reforma de Catifea: Relatiile Romaniei cu Consiliul Europei," *Sfera politicii*, June–July 1993, pp. 12–13.

13 Adrian Nastase, "The Parliamentary Dimension of the European Integration," *Romanian Journal of International Affairs*, December 1996, p. 22.

14 Napoleon Pop, "Relatiile Romaniei cu Comunitatile Europene," *Sfera politicii*, January 1993, p. 20. Also see, Teodor Melescanu, "The Ascension to the European Union: The Fundamental Option of Romania's Foreign Policy," *Romanian Journal of International Affairs*, December 1996, pp. 26–30.

15 Steven D. Roper, "The European Community as an Agent of Reform: EC Admission Criteria and Romania," *The American Review of Politics*, Spring 1994, pp. 105–121.

16 Gabriela Adamesteanu, "Romanii sint in Europa, Romania nu," 22, 20–26 March 1996, p. 11.

17 Dan Ionescu, "Romania Signs Association Accord with the EC," *RFE/RL Research Report*, 5 March 1993, p. 34.

18 Marian Chiriac, "Romania la portile Uniunii Europene," 22, 11–17 January 1995, p. 16.

19 Adrian Nastase, "The Parliamentary Dimension of the European Integration," p. 24.

20 Constantin Ene, "Accession to the European Union: Concepts and Procedures," *Romanian Journal of International Affairs*, December 1996, pp. 17–18.

21 Teodor Melescanu, "The National Security of Romania: Priorities and Legitimate Concerns," pp. 20–21.

22 Matyas Szabo, "'Historic Reconciliation' Awakens Old Disputes," p. 47.

23 Gabriel Andreescu, "Political Manipulation at Its Best," *Transition*, 1 December 1995, pp. 46–49.

24 "Constitution Watch: Romania," *East European Constitutional Review*, Fall 1996, pp. 19–20.

25 Teodor Melescanu, "The National Security of Romania: Priorities and Legitimate Concerns," p. 26.

26 Dumitru Cioflina, "NATO and Partnership for Peace: Assessment and Perspectives," *Central European Issues*, Winter 1995/1996, p. 53.

27 Constantin Dudu Ionescu, "The International Military Relations of Romania. Bilateral Military Cooperation with NATO Members," *Romanian Journal of International Affairs*, Summer 1997, pp. 62–74.

28 For a discussion concerning the specific issues involved in the modernization of the Romanian military see, Dan Zaharia, "Procurement, Modernizing and Interoperability Priorities in Romanian Armed Forces," *Romanian Journal of International Affairs*, Summer 1997, pp. 75–84.

29 Emil Constantinescu, "Speech by H. E. Mr. Emil Constantinescu, President of Romania, to the North Atlantic Council," *Romanian Journal of International Affairs*, Summer 1997, p. 5. There was an expectation among many that NATO membership would stimulate foreign investment and in essence pay for itself.

30 Gabriela Adamesteanu, "Romanii sint in Europa, Romania nu," p. 11.

31   Constantin Ene, "NATO Enlargement: More Questions than Answers. A View from Brussels," *Romanian Journal of International Affairs*, Summer 1997, pp. 31–36.

32   William J. Perry, "George C. Marshall's Vision of a United Europe," *Romanian Journal of International Affairs*, Summer 1997, p. 11.

33   Constantin Ene, "Romania Sets Its Sights on NATO Membership," *NATO Review*, November-December 1997, pp. 8–11.

34   *OMRI Daily Digest*, 28 June 1998.

35   The area of Transnistria, however, was never historically part of Bessarabia and was not part of Greater Romania see, Charles King, "Ethnicity and Institutional Reform: The Dynamics of 'Indigenization' in the Moldovan ASSR," *Nationalities Papers*, March 1998, pp. 57–72.

36   Jeff Chinn and Steven D. Roper, "Ethnic Mobilization and Reactive Nationalism: The Case of Moldova, *Nationalities Papers*, June 1995, pp. 291–325.

37   For an excellent discussion of the development of these intellectual groups see, Irina Livezeanu, "Moldavia, 1917–1990: Nationalism and Internationalism Then and Now," *Armenian Review*, Summer/Autumn 1990, pp. 153–193.

38   Jack Gold, "Bessarabia: The Thorny 'Non-Existent' Problem," *East European Quarterly*, Spring 1979, pp. 47–74.

39   Nicolae Enciu and Ion Pavelescu, "Un miracol istoric: Renasterea romanismului in Basarabia," in Ioan Scurtu, et. al., eds., *Istoria Basarabiei de la inceputuri pana in 1998* (Bucharest: Editura Semne, 1998), pp. 288–308.

40   There was a great deal of speculation that Romania was providing military assistance to Moldova during the civil war. So far, no evidence has corroborated these claims. For a discussion of this issue see, Stuart J. Kaufman and Stephen R. Bowers, "Transnational Dimensions of the Transnistrian Conflict," *Nationalities Papers*, March 1998, pp. 129–146.

41   Dan Ionescu, "Straining Family Relations," *Transition*, 12 May 1995, p. 6.

42   Vladimir Socor, "Moldovan-Romanian Relations Are Slow to Develop," *RFE/RL Research Report*, 26 June 1992, pp. 38–45.

43   The results of this referendum were non-binding.

44   William Crowther, "Ethnic Politics and the Post-Communist Transition in Moldova," *Nationalities Papers*, March 1998, pp. 147–164.

45   Dan Ionescu, "Straining Family Relations," pp. 6–8.

46   Susan Stewart, "Ukraine's Policy Towards Ethnic Minorities," *RFE/RL Research Report*, 10 September 1993, pp. 22–29. Stewart notes that the 20% figure is probably a combination of the ethnic Romanian and the ethnic Moldovan populations in Ukraine. However because she regards this ethnic distinction as unimportant, she maintains that this figure is approximately accurate.

47   O. C. Hogea, "De nationalismul Ucrainean," *Expres*, 29 March–4 April 1994, p. 13.

Bibliography

Adamesteanu, Gabriela. "Romanii sint in Europa, Romania nu." *22*, No. 12, 318 (20–26 March 1996).

Almas, Dumitru and Ioan Scurtu. "Unirea Basarabiei cu Romania: Confirmarea internationala a acestui act istoric." In *Istoria Basarabiei de la inceputuri pana in 1998*, Ioan Scurtu, et. al., eds. Bucharest: Editura Semne, 1998.

Andreescu, Gabriel. "Political Manipulation at Its Best." *Transition*, Vol. 1, No. 22 (1 December 1995).

Bacon, Walter M., Jr. "Romania: Neo-Stalinism in Search of Legitimacy." *Current History*, Vol. 80, No. 469 (April 1981).

Berinde, Mihai. "The European Agreement—An Important Stage in the Development of Mutual Trade Relations." *Romanian Journal of International Affairs*, Vol. 2, No. 4 (December 1996).

Brown, J. F. *The New Eastern Europe: The Khrushchev Era and After*. New York: Prager, 1966.

Caster, Mircea and Petre Barbu. "Monopolul electricitatii isi pierde energia." *Capital*, Vol. 6, No. 8 (27 February 1997).

Campeanu, Pavel. "Sondaje de decembrie: Decembrie '89 versiunea lui decembrie '95." *22*, No. 4, 310 (24–30 January 1996).

Campeanu, Pavel. "Opinia publica din Romania in campania electorala." In *Romania inainte si dupa 20 Mai*, Pavel Campeanu, Ariadna Combes and Mihnea Berindei, eds. Bucharest: Humanitas, 1991.

Chinn, Jeff and Steven D. Roper. "Ethnic Mobilization and Reactive Nationalism: The Case of Moldova." *Nationalities Papers*, Vol. 23, No. 2 (June 1995).

Chiriac, Marian. "Romania la portile Uniunii Europene." *22*, No. 2, 257 (11–17 January 1995).

Cioaranescu, George. "Rumania After Czechoslovakia: Ceausescu Walks the Tightrope." *East Europe*, Vol. 18, No. 6 (June 1969).

Cioflina, Dumitru. "NATO and Partnership for Peace: Assessment and Perspectives." *Central European Issues*, Vol. 1, No. 2 (Winter 1995/1996).

Cismarescu, Michael. "Rumania's Industrial Development." *East Europe*, Vol. 19, No. 1 (January 1970).

Combes, Ariadna and Mihnea Berindei. "Analiza alegelior." In *Romania inainte si dupa 20 Mai*, Pavel Campeanu, Ariadna Combes and Mihnea Berindei, eds. Bucharest: Humanitas, 1991.

Constantinescu, Emil. "Speech by H. E. Mr. Emil Constantinescu, President of Romania, to the North Atlantic Council." *Romanian Journal of International Affairs*, Vol. 3, No. 2 (Summer 1997).

Crowther, William. "Ethnic Politics and the Post-Communist Transition in Moldova." *Nationalities Papers*, Vol. 26, No. 1 (March 1998).

Crowther, William. "'Ceausescuism' and Civil-Military Relations in Romania." *Armed Forces and Society*, Vol. 15, No. 2 (Winter 1989).

Daianu, Daniel. "Dilemmas of the Stabilization Policy in Romania." *Sfera politicii*, Vol. 1, No. 5 (April 1993).

Deletant, Dennis. *Romania sub regimul comunist*. Bucharest: Civic Academy Foundation, 1997.

Earle, John S. "Unemployment Policies in Romania (II)." *Sfera politicii*, Vol. 3, No. 14 (February 1994).

Earle, John S. "Unemployment Policies in Romania." *Sfera politicii*, Vol. 3, No. 13 (January 1994).

Enciu, Nicolae and Ion Pavelescu. "Un miracol istoric: Renasterea romanismului in Basarabia." In *Istoria Basarabiei de la inceputuri pana in 1998*, Ioan Scurtu, et. al., eds. Bucharest: Editura Semne, 1998.

Ene, Constantin. "Romania Sets Its Sights on NATO Membership." *NATO Review*, Vol. 45, No. 6 (November-December 1997).

Ene, Constantin. "NATO Enlargement: More Questions than Answers. A View from Brussels." *Romanian Journal of International Affairs*, Vol. 3, No. 2 (Summer 1997).

Ene, Constantin. "Accession to the European Union: Concepts and Procedures." *Romanian Journal of International Affairs*, Vol. 2, No. 4 (December 1996).

Enescu, C. "Semnificatia alegerilor din decembrie 1937 in evolutia politica a neamului Romanesc." In *Renaterea unei democratii alegerile din Romania de la 20 mai 1990*, Petre Datculescu and Klaus Liepelt, eds. Bucharest: IRSOP, 1991.

Farlow, Robert L. "Romania: The Politics of Autonomy." *Current History*, Vol. 77, No. 452 (April 1978).

Fischer, Mary Ellen. *Nicolae Ceausescu: A Study in Political Leadership*. Boulder, CO: Lynne Rienner, 1989.

Fischer, Mary Ellen. "The Romanian Communist Party and Its Central Committee: Patterns of Growth and Change." *Southeastern Europe*, Vol. 6, No. 1 (June 1979).

Fischer-Galati, Stephen. *Twentieth Century Rumania*, 2nd ed. New York: Columbia University Press, 1991.

Fischer-Galati, Stephen. "Rumania and the Sino-Soviet Conflict." In *Eastern Europe in Transition*, Kurt London, ed. Baltimore, MD: The Johns Hopkins University Press, 1966.

Fischer-Galati, Stephen. "Rumania: A Dissenting Voice in the Balkans." In *Issues of World Communism*, Andrew Gyorgy, ed. Princeton, NJ: Van Nostrand Co., 1966.

Floyd, David. *Rumania: Russia's Dissident Ally*. New York: Praeger, 1965.

Galatanu, Mihail. "Romania este paradisul muncii la negru." *Capital*, Vol. 6, No. 46 (20 November 1997).

Gallagher, Tom. "Ultranationalists Take Charge of Transylvania's Capital." *RFE/RL Research Reports*, Vol. 1, No. 13 (27 March 1992).

Gilberg, Trond. *Nationalism and Communism in Romania: The Rise and Fall of Ceausescu's Personal Dictatorship*. Boulder, CO: Westview Press, 1991.

Gilberg, Trond. "The Communist Party of Romania." In *The Communist Parties of Eastern Europe*, Stephen Fischer-Galati, ed. New York: Columbia University Press, 1979.

Giurescu, Dinu C. *Guvernarea Nicolae Radescu*. Bucharest: Editura All, 1996.

Gold, Jack. "Bessarabia: The Thorny 'Non-Existent' Problem." *East European Quarterly*, Vol. 13, No. 1 (Spring 1979).

Grindea, Dan. *Shock Therapy and Privatization: An Analysis of Romania's Economic Reform*. New York: Columbia University Press, 1997.

Gyorgy, Andrew. "The Internal Political Order." In *Eastern Europe in the Sixties*, Stephen Fischer-Galati, ed. New York: Prager, 1963.

Hitchens, Keith. *Romania 1866–1947*. Oxford: Clarendon Press, 1994.

Iliescu, Crisan and Cristina Roman. "Sintezele platformelor electorale ale partidelor care au obtinut peste 1% din voturi." In *Renaterea unei democratii alegerile din Romania de la 20 mai 1990*, Petre Datculescu and Klaus Liepelt, eds. Bucharest: IRSOP, 1991.

Iliescu, Ion. *Romania in Europe and in the World*. Bucharest: Romania Publishers, 1994.

Ion, Liviu. "Reforma de Catifea: Relatiile Romaniei cu Consiliul Europei." *Sfera politicii*, Vol. 1, No. 7 (June-July 1993).

Ionescu, Constantin Dudu. "The International Military Relations of Romania. Bilateral Military Cooperation with NATO Members." *Romanian Journal of International Affairs*, Vol. 3, No. 2 (Summer 1997).

Ionescu, Dan. "Straining Family Relations." *Transition*, Vol. 1, No. 7 (12 May 1995).

Ionescu, Dan. "Romania Signs Association Accord with the EC." *RFE/RL Research Report*, Vol. 2, No. 9 (5 March 1993).

Ionescu, Dan. "Another Front for Romania's Salvation." *RFE/RL Research Report*, Vol. 1, No. 33 (21 August, 1992).

Ionescu, Dan. "Romania's Ruling Party Splits after Congress." *RFE/RL Research Report*, Vol. 1, No. 16 (17 April 1992).

Ionescu, Dan. "Infighting Shakes Romania's Ruling Party." *RFE/RL Research Report*, Vol. 1, No. 14 (3 April 1992).

Ionescu, Ghita. *Communism in Rumania: 1944–1962*. Oxford: Oxford University Press, 1964.

Isarescu, Mugur. "Monetary Policy, Macroeconomic Stabilization and Banking Reform in Romania 1995." *Central European Issues*, Vol. 1, No. 2 (Winter 1995/1996).

Isarescu, Mugur Constantin. "Monetary Policy and Inter-Enterprise Arrears in Romania." *Sfera politicii*, Vol. 1, No. 1 (December 1992).

Jurca, Nicolae. *Social democratia in Romania*. Sibiu: Editura Hermann, 1993.

Kaufman, Stuart J. and Stephen R. Bowers. "Transnational Dimensions of the Transnistrian Conflict." *Nationalities Papers*, Vol. 26, No. 1 (March 1998).

King, Charles. "Ethnicity and Institutional Reform: The Dynamics of 'Indigenization' in the Moldovan ASSR." *Nationalities Papers*, Vol. 26, No. 1 (March 1998).

King, Robert R. *History of the Romanian Communist Party*. Stanford, CA: Hoover Institution Press, 1980.

King, Robert R. "Romania and the Third World." *Orbis*, (Winter 1978).

Khrushchev, N.S. "Vital Questions of the Development of the World Socialist System." *The Current Digest of the Soviet Press*, Vol. 14, No. 36 (3 October 1962).

Lendvai, Paul. *Eagles in the Cobwebs: Nationalism and Communism in the Balkans*. Garden City, NY: Doubleday, 1969.

Linz, Juan J. and Alfred Stepan. *Problems of Democratic Transition and Consolidation: Southern Europe, South America, and Post-Communist Europe*. Baltimore, MD: The Johns Hopkins University Press, 1996.

Livezeanu, Irina. *Cultural Politics in Greater Romania: Regionalism, Nation Building, and Ethnic Struggle, 1918–1930*. Ithaca, NY: Cornell University Press, 1995.

Livezeanu, Irina. "Moldavia, 1917–1990: Nationalism and Internationalism Then and Now." *Armenian Review*, Vol. 43, No. 2–3 (Summer/Autumn 1990).

Maitland, Edward. "Romania's Environmental Crisis." In *To Breathe Free*, Joan DeBardeleben, ed. Washington D.C.: Woodrow Wilson Center, 1991.

Manoilescu, Mihail. *Distatul de la Viena: Memorii iulie-august 1940*. Bucharest: Editura Enciclopedica, 1991.

Melescanu, Teodor. "The Ascension to the European Union: The Fundamental Option of Romania's Foreign Policy." *Romanian Journal of International Affairs*, Vol. 2, No. 4 (December 1996).

Melescanu, Teodor. "The National Security of Romania: Priorities and Legitimate Concerns." *Central European Issues*, Vol. 1, No. 1 (Autumn 1995).

Montias, John Michael. *Economic Development in Communist Rumania*. Cambridge, MA: M.I.T. Press, 1967.

Montias, John Michael. "Background and Origins of the Rumanian Dispute with Comecon." *Soviet Studies*, Vol. 16, No. 2 (October 1964).

Nastase, Adrian. "The Parliamentary Dimension of the European Integration." *Romanian Journal of International Affairs*, Vol. 2, No. 4 (December 1996).

Neagoe, Stelian. *Istoria guvernelor Romaniei*. Bucharest: Editura Machiavelli, 1995.

Nelson, Daniel N. "Romania." In *The Legacies of Communism in Eastern Europe*, Zoltan Barany and Ivan Volgyes, eds. Baltimore, MD: The Johns Hopkins University Press, 1995.

Oltay Edith. "Minority Rights Still an Issue in Hungarian-Romanian Relations." *RFE/RL Research Report*, Vol. 1, No. 12 (20 March 1992).

Perry, William J. "George C. Marshall's Vision of a United Europe." *Romanian Journal of International Affairs*, Vol. 3, No. 2 (Summer 1997).

Pilon, Juliana Geran. *The Bloody Flag: Post-Communist Nationalism in Eastern Europe*. New Brunswick, NJ: Transaction Publishers, 1992.

Pop, Napoleon. "Relatiile Romaniei cu Comunitatile Europene." *Sfera politicii*, Vol. 1, No. 2 (January 1993).

Preda, Eugen. "Vecinii vecinilor nostri sunt ca si vecinii nostri." *Sfera politicii*, Vol. 1, No. 11 (November 1993).

Radocea, Alexandru. "Economic Revival—Prerequisite of Romania's Integration into European Structures." *Romanian Journal of International Affairs*, Vol. 2, No. 4 (December 1996).

Ratesh, Nestor. *Romania: The Entangled Revolution*. Westport, CT: Prager, 1991.

Remington, Robin. *The Warsaw Pact: Case Studies in Communist Conflict Resolution.* Cambridge, MA: M.I.T. Press, 1971.

Remington, Robin Alison. *Winter in Prague Spring: Documents on Czechoslovak Communism in Crisis.* Cambridge, MA: M.I.T. Press, 1969.

Roper, Steven D. "The Romanian Revolution from a Theoretical Perspective."*Communist and Post Communist Studies*, Vol. 27, No. 4 (December 1994).

Roper, Steven D. "The European Community as an Agent of Reform: EC Admission Criteria and Romania." *The American Review of Politics*, Vol. 15 (Spring 1994).

Roper, Steven D. and William Crowther. "The Institutionalization of the Romanian Parliament: A Case Study of the State-Building Process in Eastern Europe." *Southeastern Political Review*, Vol. 26, No. 2 (June 1998).

Sava, Dan. "Progresul technic-factor de baza in dezvoltarea intensiva a industriei." *Revista economica*, Vol. 21, No. 12 (December 1985).

Scurtu, Ioan. *Viata politica din Romania: 1918–1944* . Bucharest: Editura Albatros, 1982.

Scurtu, Ioan Scurtu and Constantin Hlihor. *Complot impotriva Romaniei.* Bucharest: Editura Academiei de Inalte Studii Militare, 1994.

Scurtu, Ioan, Gheorghe I. Ionita and Stefania Dinu. "Ocuparea Basarabiei de catre Armata Rosie. Statutul Basarabiei in cadrul Uniunii Sovietice." In *Istoria Basarabiei de la inceputuri pana in 1998*, Ioan Scurtu, et. al., eds. Bucharest: Editura Semne, 1998.

Shafir, Michael. "Romania's Road to 'Normalcy.'" *Journal of Democracy*, Vol. 8, No. 2 (April 1997).

Shafir, Michael. "Opting for Political Change." *Transition, Vol. 2*, No. 26 (27 December 1996).

Shafir, Michael. "Democratic Convention of Romania About to Split?" *OMRI Daily Digest* (20 February 1995).

Shafir Michael. "The Congress of the Hungarian Democratic Federation of Romania: Postponed Confrontations." *Sfera politicii*, Vol. 1, No. 3 (February 1993).

Shafir, Michael. "Romania's Elections: Why the Democratic Convention Lost." *RFE/RL Research Report*, Vol. 1, No. 44 (30 October 1992).

Shafir, Michael. "'War of the Roses' in Romania's National Salvation Front." *RFE/RL Research Report*, Vol. 1, No. 4 (24 January 1992).

Shafir, Michael. *Romania: Politics, Economics and Society.* Boulder, CO: Lynne Reinner Publishers, 1985.

Shafir, Michael and Dan Ionescu. "Radical Change in Romania." *Transition*, Vol. 3, No. 2 (7 February 1997).

Simion, Liana. "Do We Still Have the Green Light?" *Invest Romania*, Vol. 2, No. 8 (Summer 1998).

Slay, Ben. "External Transformation in the Post-Communist Economies: Overview and Progress." In *Russia & Eastern Europe After Communism: The Search for New Political, Economic, and Security Systems*, Michael Kraus and Ronald D. Liebowitz, eds. Boulder, CO: Westview Press, 1996.

Socor, Vladimir. "Moldovan-Romanian Relations Are Slow to Develop." *RFE/RL Research Report*, Vol. 1, No. 26 (26 June 1992).

Socor, Vladimir. "Foreign Policy in 1990." *RFE: Report on Eastern Europe*, (28 December 1990).

Socor, Vladimir. "Pastor Tokes and the Outbreak of the Revolution in Timisoara." *RFE: Report on Eastern Europe* (2 February, 1990).

Staar, Richard F. *Communist Regimes in Eastern Europe*, 3rd ed. Stanford, CA: Hoover Institution Press, 1977.

Stan, Lavinia, ed. *Romania in Transition.* Aldershot: Dartmouth Publishing, 1997.

Stefanescu, Domnita. *Cinci ani din isoria Romaniei.* Bucharest: Editura Masina de scris, 1995.

Szabo, Maytas. "'Historic Reconciliation' Awakens Old Disputes." *Transition*, Vol. 2, No. 5 (8 March 1996).

Tismaneanu, Vladimir. "The Road to Cominform: Internationalism, Factionalism, and National Communism in Romania, 1944–1948." *Sfera politicii*, Vol. 1, No. 1 (December 1992).

Tismaneanu, Vladimir. "The Revival of Politics in Romania." In *The New Europe: Revolution in East-West Relations*, Nils H. Wessell, ed. New York: The Academy of Political Science, 1991.

Tismaneanu, Vladimir. "Ceausescu's Socialism." *Problems of Communism*, Vol. 345, No. 1 (January/February 1985).

Verdery, Katherine and Gail Klingman. "Romania after Ceausescu: Post-Communist Communism?" In *Eastern Europe in Revolution*, Ivo Banac, ed. Ithaca, NY: Cornell University Press, 1992.

Index